enoughness.

THE JOURNEY TO DISCOVERING WHO YOU ALREADY ARE

DR. TARA JENKINS

Cover and type design by DIDmedia.com

Published by inspired people LLC

Published February 2020

1 2 3 3 5 6 7 8 9 0

ISBN #978-0-9846533-7-9

Printed and distributed in the US by Lightning Source, Inc.

US $22.00

THIS BOOK IS DEDICATED TO:

//

My Family! My #1 Cheering Squad!

Who Always Believe In My Enoughness Even In My Days Of Personal Doubt

My Incomparable Mother, Margaret Rawls

My Genius Husband, Charles Jenkins

My Extraordinary Children,

Charles Jenkins, III

Paris Victoria & Princess Alexandria

TABLE OF CONTENTS

THROUGH THE JOURNEY

//

> *"For we are His workmanship, created in Christ Jesus for good works,*
> *which God prepared beforehand that we should walk in them."*
> *Ephesians 2:10*

Have you ever wondered what to say in response to the following two simple words? Introduce Yourself. Each one of us has been put in that awkward meeting setting in which we are asked to go around the room and introduce ourselves to the group. Your mouth gets dry. You start pondering possible verbiage. Some people in the room have it down to a science and some stumble over a few sentences that say very little. Which are you? When you think about it, who are you, really? It doesn't seem like a complicated question and yet, for many of us, when we think about who we are, we do not know what to say. I can imagine you are rattling off some defining elements about yourself in your head: your name, your age, what neighborhood you are from, what schools you attended, child of, spouse of, parent to...we all have those preset answers. I am sure you do, too. The answers we've compiled over the years, we've been taught to say since we were able to learn.

The culture in which we live dictates labels that are applied to us before we even know how to spell our own names. At the moment of your mom's positive pregnancy test, "bun in the oven" or "pea in a pod" became the first labels attached to you. From that point on, our parents or loved ones gave us a name based on some set of reasons. In my case, I was given the name, "Tara," by my grandmother who thought a character on the soap opera, "All My Children" by that same name was sweet. For you, maybe your name was chosen from a book of baby name possibilities. Maybe you were named after your mother or father, an aunt or uncle, or possibly a grandparent or great-grandparent. I know people who were named after famous people, bridges, even streets! However it happened, suddenly you have labels at only "hours"old. Your gender - your name - and perhaps even some detail about your birth order: the youngest, the oldest, the middle child or twin began the process of defining "who you are."

As we reflect on our earliest memories, as toddlers, we are taught to say our name and our age to impress onlookers in grocery store aisles. "Can you tell the nice lady how old you are?" Responsively, our tiny hands hold up two fingers – maybe three – and we are applauded for our cuteness and unbelievable intelligence at whatever age we are at that time. We grin because basically, our goal in life is to make an intended audience happy. Whether that's the audience of our Mom, Dad, grandparents, or a store stranger, we long to make someone who's looking applaud and approve.

I remember those moments as a child, and I've definitely perpetuated this behavior as a parent. I recall loving the way our only son cutely said the number "eight."

We would tell him to say "eight" to whatever question we asked. We would then create these ridiculous math problems that all had the answer "eight." We would then say (and record when possible), "Charles, what is the answer to 2,020 minus 2,012?" (or whatever math problem we created). At the moment that he answered "eight," all surrounding family and friends would explode in cheers and wows. This type of parenting, I'm sure, introduces the notion of crowd pleasing, as well. When we think about it, who doesn't want to be a crowd pleaser? It is so much better than not pleasing the crowd, right?

Some of the first outfits we wear are based on the preferences of a parent, grandparent, or maybe even a Godparent until the magical day we recognize that we can speak up without sponsoring a thread that we have on and possibly change that aspect of ourselves. I distinctly remember being the only person that looked the way that I looked in Mrs. Stanley's first-grade class which was a split class with second graders. From the first day of first grade when she went on and on about how cute my outfit was and let me walk around with her all day, I had a goal of getting that compliment from her everyday. I began to imagine her voice when I was getting dressed in the morning. I recall one morning my mom had dressed me in a peach polo style shirt which had one tiny flower on it. I immediately thought this outfit was too plain for Mrs. Stanley's taste. I then said to my mom, "Mama, Mrs. Stanley is not gonna say that I look cute today." See, even then, as a first-grader, I knew that Mrs. Stanley was important. Not only was she the first & second-grade teacher at Andrew Jackson Elementary School in Jackson, Tennessee, she was also the wife of the Superintendent of the entire City School System. My awareness of this at that age is surprising to me now even as I trace my own steps of searching for *enough-*

ness. Perhaps, this early memory is when my appetite for approval was awakened.

Think about it. As each of us grows older, our focus on acceptance continues with a desire to receive approval from a growing audience of peers, teachers, coaches, co-workers, love interests, then spouses, and children. Throughout our developmental years, we are constantly reminded how valued performance is academically, athletically, and artistically. We began to measure our own importance and the importance of others on achievement, and if we are not careful and cautious. our ideals become idols. Intentionally or unknowingly, we can deify a modeled image or a certain status as we long to belong. If we don't measure up to this ideal we've placed value on in some way, we can enter a cycle of processing perceived failure, which breeds condemnation, judgment, and insecurity. Left unchecked, the narratives which began from day one until now, dictate and define every aspect of our being. We believe, become, or adapt to the person all aspects of society tells us we are. Moreover, we insist upon reiterating in our mirror every morning what we've been told to believe, be it positive or negative, whatever it may be.

In preparation for writing this book, I thought of my canned responses to this simple yet extremely complicated question, "Who are you?" I am Tara Yvette Rawls Jenkins, daughter to Margaret Rawls and the late George Rawls, wife of Charles Jenkins, mother to Princess Alexandria, Paris Victoria, and Charles Jenkins III. At the moment that I'm writing this book, I am 44 years old. I have degrees from Clark Atlanta University, Moody Bible Institute, and Southern Baptist Theological Seminary. I grew up in Jackson, Tennessee, but for the past 22 years, Chicago has been my home. In most of the settings I've served, over the past 20 years, I've been introduced as the pastor's wife at Fellowship Missionary Baptist Church of Chicago and that role and identifier is ending as my husband is set to retire at the end of the calendar year.

So, WHO AM I? You've read that I'm their child, his wife and their mom, this city's native and that city's resident, and I could continue to give you more credentials according to what I've done or who I belong with. The problem is, I still have not told you WHO I am. I've told you who I am to others. I've told you what I have done. Essentially, I've told you about my labels. Realistically, how often do we know WHO we are apart from our labels? It's as if we have to read our own name tags to describe ourselves.

I know a lady who goes on a ski trip every year. For whatever reason, she keeps her resort tags, you know the ones that allow you on and off the lifts and are attached to the zipper of your ski jacket? At any given moment, she could have 20 dangling from her coat. And she loves it! I like to think of our labels in the same way, dangling from every part of us, and not necessarily in a good way. The more we accept, the more they begin to add up. How many of those labels represent us and how many of them are simply labels we've accepted because someone placed them on us.

God sees you and me as so much more than those labels attached to our zippers. We are more than the sum of our accumulated experiences: memories, desires, beliefs, successes, failures, knowledge, sensations, joys and sorrows. These perceived 'wins' or 'losses' may be things that attached themselves to you, but they are not you! Assigned attachments do not define 'who' you are.

Have you ever examined a watch? It is made up of a face, hands, battery or crown (depending upon if it is self-winding or not), the crystal, and band. Some watches have more parts and therefore have a higher price tag than others. However, we understand that the watch is a watch, created to tell time. It is not a watch first and attachments added. The face, hands, battery, crown, crystal, and the band make up the watch as a whole - collectively. The intricate details of telling time stem from the initial creation of the 'watch'. Its inventor made it explicitly for a definitive reason – to tell time. The watch was no accident. It had a distinct purpose at the moment of design. You have a purpose that is more important than any attachment placed on you academically, legally or relationally.

There is something so much more to you than the labels that have been placed on you. The Bible tells us that God was speaking to Jeremiah, and He told him, "Before I formed you in the womb, I knew you; before you were born, I set you apart…" – Jeremiah 1:5. This isn't just for Jeremiah but for you and for me. Before we were a zygote, God knew WHO we were. He set us apart for a specific task, a particular purpose, a distinct role in His story. You are not an accident and you are certainly not a mistake. While you may have been a surprise to your parents, you were no surprise to God. You have a unique spot in the universe that only YOU can fill. You matter. You alone matter. You matter today…right now. No decision or flaw changes the fact that you are important and unique to God. You have a place suitable for the time in which you are living. And, most importantly, you matter to the Creator of the Universe.

So why, at times, does it seem so difficult to live out who we are? How do we find ourselves stuck on the treadmill of life, tired with no change of scenery, running fast but going nowhere? My best friend Phillis often says that you can live life with a lot of motion but no movement. Yet, with all of this exertion, many of us still live lives tired from fruitless effort, feeling unfulfilled, unnecessary, pretending our days away. We often pretentiously become people we can't even identify as ourselves.

When you discover who you really are – who God created you to be – the guess-work of wondering what you should do or how you should act simply evaporates. It is the driving force behind writing this book because I know the huge advantage of answering this universal question. Every morning I stand before my mirror and re-mind myself of "Who I Am," and WHO AM I? ***ENOUGH!*** No longer do I conform to whom others say I should be but find fulfillment in who God designed me to be.

Realizing the clear intent of God's blueprint for your life dissolves your confu-sion, all of your fears, and insecurities. There is no longer any measuring yourself against others—or being confined by the box society has built around you. As you become who you were divinely purposed to be, you find freedom in who you are! Your impact on the world starts to unfold... and every new morning brings the ful-fillment you've wanted all your life.

You are embarking on a journey to become the person at your core – the person God purposed long before you were a twinkle in your parents' eyes. At the very essence of you is the person you've always been: a unique, custom-built child of God with a powerful, eternal purpose; but finding the "true you" can be challeng-ing. Peeling back the layers of labels takes time, truth, and work. The narratives which others continually project on us as we go along each day can debilitate us, reminding us of what we lack or how little we are compared to others. We accept the person others prefer us to be and begin to reason away the possibility of being who we've been told we could never be. The result? We walk the way we've been told to walk—but we're stuck on a circular path of life which leads to the same place every day.

Today, everything changes! The challenge begins with your opening the pages of this book. It is time to fill your heart and mind with the *enoughness* of who you are in Jesus Christ-- Who, through His love, has perfectly proportioned within you every talent, every task, every skill you need to become the person you were created and intended to be!

The *enoughness* of our creation allows us to stop the deception which tells us who we are NOT or who we are pretending to be --and permits us to see clearly WHO we really ARE. Deposited within you and me is a rich, bold, and deeply meaningful future, but we must allow God access to withdraw it!

As we explore the possibilities together, I want you to take a moment and consider this sentence, "I am who God says I am. I am *ENOUGH*." Write it on your mirror; place it on an index card in your car; put it on a sticky note on your desk at work, or by your bedside table. As we grow through the pages of this book and through God, you will learn to add much-needed words to complete your identity in Him. "I am *ENOUGH* because God says I am. I am beautiful because God says I am. I am loving, kind, responsive, nurturing because God says I am. I am protected. I am healed. I am victorious because God says I am."

Are you ready to open up your heart to the person God already made you to be and not the labels you've grown accustomed to being? This is not a self-help book nor am I making promises about a better you in a certain amount of time. There is no special formula or step-by-step directives. What I do want to offer you is the opportunity to feel fulfilled; to have an impact on the world; to embrace the joy that comes from being who you are, and to develop a deep connection with your Creator.

So, if you are tired of trying to find meaning and direction…if you are weary from wondering what you were meant to do…if you feel stuck in an ordinary life… *enoughness* will guide you to your core, your created self, the "ENOUGHNESS " zone in which you were intended to live.

THROUGH THE JOURNEY:
LET'S TAKE IT PERSONAL THEN
LET'S MAKE IT SPIRITUAL

Imagine new items you may purchase. A frame for a picture, a cute set of jars that you can fill with florals or candles. Each is ready for display or use except for one thing, the store price sticker. Recently, my family and I took some family photos. I thought the pictures were ready to send out until I realized a blaring obvious price sticker that was showing on the bottom of my shoe! That one detail was a distraction. That one label blemished the image I was set to send out. Some stickers easily peel off. Others peel off partly, and you can still see part of the price tag. Then others are stubborn and will not come off. Together, let's deal with some label removal.

THINKING IT THROUGH

What labels do you wear? _____

_____

_____

What labels have you peeled off that you think may have left residue behind? ____

_____

_____

What labels do you feel stuck with? _____

_____

_____

What labels are important to you or have significant meaning? _____

_____

HOW YOU VIEW YOURSELF IS OFTEN REVEALED IN HOW YOU INTRODUCE YOURSELF.

Take A Moment: Reflect and write out how you usually introduce yourself in new settings or with new people. Through this exercise you will see what labels have been sticking to you and which ones you need to work on peeling off.

THINKING IT THROUGH

Who Are You?_____

_____

_____

What Do You Do? _____

_____

_____

Where Are You From? _____

_____

_____

CANNED RESPONSE vs CANDID REVISIT

What I Say   What's My Truth

NEVER ENOUGH

> *"You alone created my inner being. You knitted me together inside my mother. I will give thanks to you because I have been so amazingly and miraculously made. Your works are miraculous, and my soul is fully aware of this."*
> Psalm 139:13-14

If you were given the opportunity to describe the kind of person you are, what would you say? What characteristics make you unique? What makes you different from anyone else? What do you like most about yourself? What do you dislike the most about yourself?

We've learned to view ourselves through the lenses of others. A friend of mine, whom I love dearly, got to a low point in her life where she had to make the hard decision to fast from social media until she was emotionally healthy enough to be online in that way. My husband often says that social media is a brick. You can build something with it or you can tear something down with it.

The reality of social media is, it fills our lives in so many ways with positive connections. I have reconnected with people I would never have been able to without social media. I've also been able to pray with those who have needs that I would never have known about because of distance or loss of contact. Seeing and celebrating with family and friends is fun. Wishing people a "Happy Anniversary" or "Happy Birthday" brings smiles. But, there is a negative element we don't like to talk about but need to talk about. These platforms can become breeding grounds for comparisonitis and fuel our discontentment. Not only does social media cause more opportunities for comparing, but it can also be a time consumer, or should I say a *time thief*? We've become programmed to check our devices when we open our eyes: weather, news, emails, Facebook, Instagram and Twitter. I call it the ten-minute morning fix, though many of our screen times report more than 10 minutes. Similar to an addictive habit, we struggle to disconnect. There is this ongoing hovering effect, enticing us, calling us to check our devices one more time. We have a false sense of being in the know and do not want to feel any part of being left out and excluded. Could the God that woke you up actually be the one being excluded? Can you imagine God saying, "Yo, over here, speak to me first!"

Recently, I have become painfully aware of how little interaction people have with one another in person. Glance around a restaurant, a park, a coffee shop, and you will see necks bent down, hovering over devices - even when there are two people at the same table. We value the person on the other end of the electronics more than we do breathing right in front of us. And we wonder why most people in the world would say they feel insignificant? Devalued? Friendless?

We also struggle to understand why we are unable to complete tasks or concentrate. The reality of that device which we cling to and have to have in our hand or nearby 24/7, when it beeps, we look. I've learned when I am writing to put it in a draw with negotiations to check it every thirty minute (only because I have children in all different places). If I do not do that, I will be drawn into the Social Media World and away from my Heavenly Father.

Social media lures us into a false sense of reality, too. We compare our lives to those of others in a way we never have before because everything from what is being cooked for dinner, decorations in the home, new cars, children's accomplishments to perfect family gatherings are displayed 24 hours a day, seven days a week. Most people don't post the laundry piled against the wall; dirty dishes in the sink; the two-year-old meltdown in the aisle of the supermarket; or the difficulties of family dynamics in a photograph. Does anyone ever post anything REAL? We are drawn into a world of *Unreality* TV. Our obsession breeds the chronic discontent which follows our inability to disconnect. In other words, we are in a perpetual state of being "Never Enough."

Posts after posts, scroll after scroll, filter on top of filter, we are consuming lies. Lies which cause us to doubt who we are as individuals and as believers. Our measuring stick against others is far from accurate. We begin to view our life as the only life/family that isn't living the dream! The narratives which play in our minds build on the hurts and failures of our past, digging deeper wounds, shutting us out of the real person within us, the person God so beautifully created us to be. Left to our own thoughts and views, we wonder where these lies come from and why we believe them?

From day one, when we are wrapped in a blue or pink blanket, we are conformed to the ideals of society and tradition. Because my grandmother did something a particular way, my mom did it, and I'm sure I did too. We learn from watching, listening, and experiencing how those around us do life. There is nothing wrong with it, for it is the process of learning. I remember watching how my mother made her bed; how she added pillows on pillows on pillows; how she tucked the sheets in and pulled the comforter back to make it look pretty. I still define a properly "made bed" the same way. We mimic what we see; and we digest the echoes we hear.

Through Pre-School and into Elementary school, society shows us how the status quo acts, what is normal, and what is expected if we are to be accepted. And, as long as we are following those guidelines, we are good; but, not all of us are equipped to do so. As we build on those expectations, the criteria which tells us we are accepted or not accepted, we fall further into the trap of labels and further away from the person God created and intended us to be.

My strong and no nonsense mom filed for divorce when she was seven months pregnant with me. However, although I grew up without my father in my home, I never felt a lack of love or family support in any way. My Aunt Liz moved in and helped raise me until she got married when I was 11. I have always been surrounded by a supportive family from my mother's side and also from the family of my mostly absent father. I didn't know anything about my family "structure" wasn't considered *normal* by society's standards until one day I was playing outside with a friend who said, "I'm not from a broken home like you." Broken home? Because of the incredible family support and network of my mom, I never knew I was missing a father or that anything was broken in my life.

In my family growing up, I was surrounded by stability and love. I am so grateful for the roots which grounded me by my grandmother, grandfather, uncles, aunts, cousins, Godparents and my mom. Any event in which I was involved, I had a cheering section of family. I praise God for my family and the power that equipped them to compensate for any potential lack, and how they made it "work" for our family. As you read this, I understand that you may or may not have had a similar background. Your story may be different from mine. Perhaps, in your upbringing, you felt the brokenness and instability from a one parent home or a no parent home. Maybe you had both parents but an absence of love. In all of us, there are empty gaps, no matter how conventional or unconventional we were raised. Those empty places need filling and healing. They need to be recognized and dealt with. We all tuck emotions away which we no longer want to feel; but, you have to feel it to heal it. In some cases, you have to find it first and drag it out.

Our early years play a huge part in our development and our ability to find out who we were intended to be. Maybe, even though you had support all around you, the differentness of your life made others point out what or who you weren't or what you didn't have. These words have created a narrative for your life which plays on your feeling of *not-enoughness*. There is something within every one of us which nudges, prys, pokes, and pricks those places which breed inadequacy and incompetence.

God can give you, grant you, and grace you with the feeling of fulfillment and *enoughness*, even when the statistics or current status of your life appears like a *less-than-enough* situation. Our inner being was created by God to fulfill purpose in His Kingdom. Our inner selves listen to the calling of God, but our flesh ignores or does not want to accept it. While so many of us live as if those words of purpose and plan sound good and we like the idea of it, we do not always live as if we believe it. As we mature and navigate through life, we can begin to (by default) conform ourselves more and more to who the world tells us we are and not who God tells us we are.

As a speaker, I often ask audiences, "How many of you remember being young and sharing what you wanted to be *when you grow up*?" When we reflect back on who we wanted to be, how many of us are doing exactly what we originally dreamed? Usually, the majority who answer the question has had a plan change since that original desire. Which leads to the second question, "How many of us are participating in something we are passionate about? How many of us feel like we are living a life which we have succumbed to?"

When we step back and look at our current lives, we realize we have settled for much less than what God intended, and our lives are not what we desired either. God wants us to live the life He planned for us, not just some life we are resolved to have based on making the people around us comfortable or conforming to a mold someone told us to step into.

One of my favorite stories in the Bible comes from 1 Kings 19. It begins with a well-known prophet of the day named Elijah. Elijah lived a pretty amazing life - and if drama is something you enjoy, tune in to Elijah's life! He appears as if he is a nobody from nowhere, without a long lineage of descendants in the first half of the ninth century BCE; however, Elijah was covered with the amazing power of God.

In 1 Kings 19, after a huge win against the prophets of Baal, calling rain down from the sky after years of drought, he finds himself on the run for his life because King Ahab's wife, Queen Jezebel, wants his head. In the first few verses of 1 King 19, Elijah is sitting under a broom brush asking God to allow him to die.

> *"'I have had enough, Lord,' he said. 'Take my life; I am no better than my ancestors.' Then he lay down under the bush and fell asleep."*
> *1 Kings 19: 4-5.*

Have you ever felt that way? Weary from the trials of life - lost under a broom bush - exhausted? Have you ever felt like a failure, with no purpose, and no direction? Well, you are in good company because this is exactly how Elijah felt. Even after big victories, he finds himself in a posture praying to die.

An angel of the Lord touches his shoulder to awaken him. He is told to eat and drink for he will need to strengthen himself for the journey. Elijah wakes up, eats, and falls back to sleep. He is later awakened a second time by the angel. He eats and begins the journey God has called him to take. Of the many instructions Elijah is given, his journey will take him to appoint his successor. A man who is working in the fields totally unaware that God has a plan for his life. A man focused on his daily life, unsuspecting that Elijah the prophet is on his way to change the direction of his life.

When I read scripture, I often imagine some of the stories as musical theatre. As you may have guessed, I love theatre - musicals, concerts, and dance productions. Anyone who knows me knows I can be a bit theatrical at times. My friend Robin and I have an ongoing debate with our young kids about which mom is the most dramatic. It is currently a toss up! All in all, I just respect and admire well done productions. One of my favorite parts and points of a concert or play is the Intermission. I'm not like those who get up and stretch or go to the lobby for coffee and candy. No! I stay in my seat and listen to the sounds behind the curtain. When the black curtain falls, I am instantly intrigued. What is going to happen next? As I sit in anticipation of the possibilities, I think about God.

Sometimes, our lives are in Intermission. We don't know what God is doing behind the black curtain while we wait, but He does. We can hear that change is coming before we actually see it and in theatre, I love to hear the sets being moved as the music of the band or orchestra plays. Scenes for the upcoming Acts are being put into place for the end product - the Finale.

As we walk in our ordinary lives, God is orchestrating events behind the curtain to open the doors of our life purposes. The tough question is how many of us actually recognize or walk through those doors? Even more poignant, how many of us actually believe God is behind our life scenes? Granted, there are many scenes and portions in my own life's script that I would have fast forwarded, edited or just outright deleted. However, God continues to show us that every scene works together for a good Finale He has planned according to Romans 8:28, *"And we know that in all things God works for the good of those who love Him, who have been called according to His purpose."*

When Elijah enters the fields where Elisha works as a plow foreman of sorts, Intermission is ending and the next Act is beginning. There have been moments in my life when I have felt the movement of the Lord. I knew instantly that Intermission was ending and the next part of the story was beginning in my life. Maybe you have felt it too or are feeling this way right now. Sometimes, we don't know Intermission is over until we are well into the next Act. It all depends on Him.

"So Elijah went from there and found Elisha the son of Shaphat. He was plowing with twelve yoke of oxen, and he himself was driving the twelfth pair. Elijah went up to him and threw his cloak around him. Elisha then left his oxen and ran after Elijah. 'Let me kiss my father and mother goodbye,' he said, 'and then I will come with you.'"

There is nothing wrong with the type of work Elisha was doing daily. He worked hard and probably had a managerial type position because it says he drove the twelfth oxen pair. If he was in a supervisory position he would need to be the last team of oxen to make certain all the rows were plowed correctly. What do you think his life was like? I can imagine his day-to-day routine: get up; breakfast; get dressed; hook up his oxen team; plow, plow, plow; lunch break; water the oxen; plow, plow, plow; untack the oxen; feed them; head home; dinner; bed; start all over again. It is what Elisha did every day. While it was not ALL he was purposed to do, it was what he did while waiting to do what he was called to do. The wonderful part of the story is, when Elijah placed the cloak over Elisha's shoulders, Elisha was *ready* to respond.

> *"So Elisha left him and went back. He took his yoke of oxen and slaughtered them. He burned the plowing equipment to cook the meat and gave it to the people, and they ate. Then he set out to follow Elijah and became his servant."*
> *Kings 19:20.*

Elisha did not know Elijah was coming. He didn't know today would be the last day he would stand behind a plow of oxen. But when Elijah placed the cloak over Elisha, he knew what was happening was not ordinary. He didn't reason in his mind, "...this will be a great thing to try and if it doesn't work out, I'll just come back." His actions are much more intentional. The Bible tells us he burned his plows, slaughtered his oxen, and fed his family and friends the meat. The reality is if his plows are destroyed, his oxen are destroyed, and his family is aware of the destruction, I don't think he is coming back to work any time soon. Elisha rose to the opportunity in the moment knowing his own *enoughness* and went into his next season of purpose, full speed ahead.

Many of us have settled for a life society told us was ours because some of us were told that we were *never enough* to do or be anything else. You may feel as if you have heard the calling of God to do something more, but you do not feel as if you have *enough* of what it takes to step out and reach that calling. You may find yourself in a season when you feel like there is never enough time...never enough money...you've never had enough education...never enough support or never enough confidence to do everything that life requires from you.

Possibly, your plow isn't a physical object but a mental object. Maybe you need to burn the plows and slaughter the oxen which tell you, you will never have enough money to go to college; you will never have enough intelligence to graduate; you will never have the skills to operate a business; you will never have enough discipline to lose the weight; you will never have enough strength to kick that addiction; you will never have enough stability to be a mom; you will never have enough to overcome your past; you will never have enough to be forgiven for what you've done; you will never have enough to change; you will never have enough...

John 1:12, "*Yet to all who did receive Him, to those who believed in His name, He gave the right to become children of God.*"

Do you see yourself as the Creator's creative creation? I love saying those words, "I am the Creator's creative creation." There is something about hearing and believing that I am a creative creation of the Creator that rings in my ears and makes me want to dance. I am not ordinary. I am unique. I am different from anyone else and so are you. There is a mantra which I like to say to myself when I am feeling "less" than *enough* to do some particular feat I am facing. It is simple, but empowers me. "I don't fit in because I was born to stand out." As children of the Creator, we are purposed, unique, shining lights that stand out in a crowd and glow in every dark place. We won't fit in because we stand out!

Do you feel the certainty of being God's child, His creative creation? Do you realize that you are royalty, by virtue of the fact that you are not just A king's kid but THE King of kings' kid? Think about what that looks like. You are a child of the King of kings, the Lord of lords, the creative Creator of the Universe! The identity that you find as a child of God cannot be minimized. Your identity doesn't rise or fall according to what you do or do not do - what you look like or do not look like. As a child of the Most High God, society no longer plays a key role in who you are or how you are labeled. You can't become MORE of a child of God by merit or LESS of a child of God by mistakes. You never have *enough* good work to increase His love for you as a Father AND you never have *enough* failures to lose His love. Your identity starts here...

NEVER ENOUGH: LET'S TAKE IT PERSONAL

After an amazing childhood surrounded with individuals rooting for me, what could have felt like the end of the world for me at 17 (not graduating with my high school class) was the reality check that I didn't know I needed. Everything will not always work out the way I think it should whether that's based on my own actions or even in circumstances beyond my control. Not everyone will be encouraging, whether you are experiencing a higher than high or a lower than low point in your life. Leaving home and moving into my dorm room in Pfeiffer Hall at Clark Atlanta University was an interesting transition. I was super excited to start this journey at my first choice, an HBCU(Historically Black College/University). At the same time, entering a new city, a new setting, and a new season on the heels of this public disappointment left me with a sense of hidden shame feeling as if I were the only one coming into this setting straight from summer school. It appeared to me that everyone else had a high school graduation, with graduation pictures decorating their dorm room. When I started college, I had not seen my diploma. It came in the mail very unceremoniously while I was away.

I can reflect and admit, my outgoing, try-anything personality did mellow out some during the beginning of my matriculation through Clark Atlanta University. My first couple of semesters' grades were blah (until my mom made me drive a forklift and work shifts in a factory that summer after Freshman Year). Though filled with uncertainty for the coming semesters, my determination out weighed my doubt for I am 100% allergic to quitting.

I've always had a *don't quit* spirit. My feelings are hurt right now when my kids want to quit an activity, sport, language or instrument. I go into a chant, "The Jenkins Don't Quit! The Jenkins Don't Quit!"

Nevertheless, you may be determined and still shocked like I was that everybody does not want to see you *win*. What a bubble I was living in! But life has burst my bubble quickly and repeatedly. Relinquish the need to know why it is that some people are against you and believe that you will *never be enough*. Get on to doing what you believe God has called you to do in the place that you believe that He has called you to do it.

Don't let the empty stands, the booing chants, or the cheering fans determine your direction or obedience to God.

You are *ENOUGH* to do what God called you to do because the Lord is with you!

He made you!

He chose you!

You matter to HIS story!

YOUR *ENOUGHNESS* WILL BE DISCOVERED AS WE UNCOVER THE AREAS WHERE YOU HAVE BEEN TOLD THAT YOU ARE *NOT ENOUGH.*

What "never enoughs" have you heard an echo of in your life?

What "never enoughs" have you heard on replay in your mind?

This is our starting point. This is the before to our after.

Example:

I will never be _____focused_____ enough to _____graduate_____ .

Write Yours Below: Make It Personal!

I will never be _____ enough to _____ .

I will never be _____ enough to _____ .

I will never be _____ enough to _____ .

I will never be _____ enough to _____ .

I will never be _____ enough to _____ .

HAD ENOUGH

//

> *"But you are a chosen race, a royal priesthood, a Holy nation, a people for His own possession, that you may proclaim the excellencies of Him Who called you out of darkness into His marvelous light."*
> *1 Peter 2:9*

In the Beginning GOD...those are the words that open it all: Creation, the Bible, Life. They are the words which start Genesis 1:1, *"In the beginning, God created the Heavens and the Earth."* In reality those words should begin every day, every thought, every action we have as believers in the All Mighty God, our Creator, our Father. The Hebrew word for "In the Beginning" is *Bereshit* (תישארב תישארב), and interestingly, this word is used only in reference to God. What is real about these 4 words is it ALL started with God - it ALL is God. HE is where it all begins! He created the Heavens, the Earth and YOU! Since we are His creations, we should start each day consulting the One who created us.

How does your day start? What does your morning look like? Walk through it with me - you open your eyes after a long night's sleep or maybe a not so long sleep - maybe you couldn't sleep or it was a restless night of intermittent sleep, leaving you feeling exhausted and unmotivated to get out of bed. Forcefully, you put your feet on the ground and push your way up. Another day of endless cyclical duties-- stumbling through the day or robotically moving through it -- merely existing.

Statistically, we are told that most of us live our lives unaware as to what LIV- ING actually means. There are studies upon studies which tell us having purpose, having direction, having feelings of self-worth bring satisfaction, longevity, and value to our lives. We are people who want to know that there is much more to our lives than simply living and breathing air. Because we want to know this, we must have internally determined there is more. So, why is it so difficult to discover what the intent of our being actually is? I believe it is most difficult when we live discon- nected from clarity from our Creator.

The same Creator that created Heaven and Earth in the beginning, also created our bodies, our being and our brains. The brain is such an incredible mechanism on many levels. Though complex in creation and function, we have access to com- municate with the Creator for clarity, for our lives, and for confirmation that we are enough to do what we were created to do.

Over my last two decades in full time ministry, I have learned many unforget- table lessons. One that sticks out comes from the moments when we were called to pray over a life which was ending. Never did I witness a dying person in his or her last days wishing he/she had more money, more cars, boats, or homes. Often the words from a person who is facing their last days are, "I had so much more to do!" or "I wish I had cared less about what people thought and tried doing what I thought I was to do." Too often our lives are filled with things that are not life-giving. When reflecting on the brevity of life, we must be prompted to put forth the effort to live life in a way that gives us life and serves the purpose for which the Creator created us.

James 4:14b says, "You are just a vapor that appears for a little while and then vanishes away." What part of your life is getting in the way of you living life during your time on earth? Think about this passage in James. Life is a vapor. Picture blowing your warm breath on a mirror or glass, and just having a few seconds to write something in that glass. This is how quickly our life is within the context of eternity. What are you writing in the moments that your vapor is visible?

I remember growing up with certain individuals who seemed that they were born knowing what they would do for their entire lives. There was one guy that always declared he was going to be a doctor. Any school report he ever did was about some facet of medicine, whether it was developing a cure or going into underdeveloped countries or opening up an office right in our hometown. There were very few people like him - driven, motivated, focused. Other associates of mine changed career aspirations regularly. For me, I knew I wanted to do something in the media, but often vacillated about exactly what. I wasn't completely certain exactly what I would do, or like my friends, my interests floated from one potential life adventure to another - Broadcast Journalism? Print Journalism? Public Relations? Secular

Radio? Gospel Radio? Business Communications?

As I neared the end of my matriculation through Clark-Atlanta University, I applied to graduate school thinking I would further my communications studies, but through the application process I shifted. I was on an uncertain educational path at first. Voices around me suggested this and that. I came to terms with the fact that just because a person is able to do something well doesn't necessarily mean it is his or her calling, passion, or purpose. What started as an application to further my studies in business and corporate communications ended in a commitment to Bible school and seminary with scholarships that followed. Although my original plan was altered, I was determined to follow the Creator's interruption of my plan. To do anything else can lead us to a place where we are living life with a sense of dread with little or no direction but our own uncertainties. People often say, 'The choice is yours,' but there are moments where God's confirmation and leading is so loud, you feel that the choice has been made.

Have you ever had an unsatisfied feeling in the pit of your stomach? Perhaps that's a feeling of frustration as you dread purposelessly going to a job you care nothing about other than the paycheck; not realizing you have the *enoughness* to do something new or try something else! In retrospect, most of us can look back and realize our blindspots. When we look back on our lives, on our decisions, we can usually see what we missed. How is it we didn't see it at the time?

Psalm 16:11 tells us, "*You will make known to me the path of life; in Your presence is fullness of joy; in Your right hand there are pleasures forever.*"

"*YOU WILL...*" Those two words are so valuable to finding who you are, to finding who God intended you to be. The word "YOU" refers to God, our Heavenly

Father, our Creator, and it is a promise from Him to us. He assures us, "I WILL make known to you the path of life." Do you know the first words which should come out of our hearts when we wake up in the morning? Words that begin with Him - "God, my Father, make known my path. My day starts with You. My heart sings of You today. Give me joy, despite the difficult challenges I am facing. Give me hope, even though things look hopeless; Make my path - Your path. Make my words - Your words. Make my plan- Your plan. Make my appointments - Your appointments. Help me to Be ONE with you today."

The amazingly merciful part of God is He created us knowing we would fail Him. Since He is above time - has always been and will always be - He knows the choices we will make before we make them - He knew Adam and Eve would sin against Him; yet, He still spent time with them, walking in the garden, loving them.

Genesis 3:8-10 tells us, "*Then the man and his wife heard the voice of the LORD God...*" Can you imagine the incredible gift Adam and Eve had - God called them out by name, "Adam! Eve!" I can imagine it like my mom's unmistakable voice calling me. I could hear her all the way down the street, and you better believe I came running when she called. Adam and Eve had this unprecedented relationship in which they walked with God in the garden and talked to Him. "*...and they hid themselves from the presence of the LORD God among the trees of the garden.*" God calls out to them, "*Where are you?*"

An important part of the story is this... God knows exactly where Adam and Eve are as He calls out to them. He knows what the serpent did; He knows what Eve said; He knows Adam went along with the whole thing; and, He knew before He created Adam and Eve that this very day would come. The beautiful part is - He created them anyway.

In that same way, God knows every mistake and misstep we will make and still calls us, uses us, and refuses to give up on us. With everything we will do wrong, He still knows in His all knowingness that He created us with *enoughness* for Him to still get the glory through our stories. Despite who we say we are - despite who society tells us we are - despite who the narratives in our minds remind us that we are - He is still able to use us for His glory.

If you are a mother of more than one child reading this, think about the decision or Divine direction that led you to the point of having a second, third or more child. Despite the pain and discomfort that you knew this process included, you went forward with the childbirth experience again. It is because of the love outweighing pain that we decide on baby number 2; number 3; and some number 4 or more.

God wanted a relationship with us despite what He knew we would do. He knew we would turn His perfect plan upside down. Despite Adam and Eve and their short-comings, He created them and entered into a relationship which would lead to His Son Jesus Christ suffering and dying on the Cross to save us. Regardless of whether you are living out your calling or purpose in life, God's love comes with no conditions. You may have failed Him 100,000 times in the past with 100,000 times to come; yet, He still wants you to fulfill the purpose He intended for your life. He believes in you. You are the apple of His eye. He has purposed you to do good works. He knows what you are capable of doing. He does not buy the lies you tell yourself. You are His little love.

I remember going to Tigrett Jr. High that housed 7th through 9th grades. In my first year of junior high, a ninth grader came up to me at the end of a pep rally and said, "You think you cute!" Then she kicked me in the shin and walked away. I was so stunned that I didn't respond at all. As I think of that moment now, I realize whether you think you're cute or not, you should know that GOD DOES! You are His handiwork, artwork, prized possession and one of a kind creation. No one has your footprint, fingerprint, earshape, voice texture, gift mix or calling!

Wouldn't it be nice to open your eyes in the morning and see the intent of God for your life and moreover for your day? What is standing in your way of doing what God wanted for your life? Maybe you are presently wondering if you actually are in the life God chose for you. How do we really know one way or the other?

John 1:1-5 proclaims, "*In the beginning was the Word, and the Word was with God, and the Word was God. The same was in the beginning with God. All things were made by Him; and without Him was not anything made that was made. In Him was life; and the life was the light of men. And the light shineth in darkness; and the darkness comprehended it not.*"

I don't want to be the last six words of that scripture, "*...and the darkness comprehended it not.*" I don't want to be drifting aimlessly along in life missing what God has for me because I cannot comprehend it. The decisions that we make; the reactions which cause us to act one way or the other; the roles we play in our daily lives are all a part of how we live God-centered lives of purpose. Because of this, there are certain actions which inevitably prevent us from having the life God wants for us. Haven't you had enough of the guesswork? Had enough of the listless, passionless, stagnant day-to-day movements, never knowing who you really are? Had enough of the masks, the roles, the fake impressions, the unidentifiable person within? It is time to put that "had enough" feeling to bed and wake up with the *enoughness* feeling of Jesus Christ.

When you have 'had enough' of not feeling like enough, you will realize that you've always "HAD ENOUGH" to be everything God designed you to be. Just as the popular films *The Wizard of Oz* and adaptation *The Wiz* communicate, you have always had the power all along. You've HAD ENOUGH!

Take a look at your own life. What could be blocking you from living your life of *ENOUGHNESS*.

1. **Am I living a life with a self-sabotaging sin cycle in it?**

   Hiding, sneaking, sweeping a struggle under the rug may work for a period of time with those around you, it does not work with God. Remember His walk in the garden after Adam and Eve ate of the fruit on the tree? God knew exactly where they were. He knew exactly what they had done. And, He knew what the consequences of their sin would mean to the world. Unbelievably, He loved them anyway. You cannot fully become ALL you were intended and purposed to be, if you are living a life in intentional disobedience to God. God cannot do all He wants in your life until you recognize and reach for obedience. If you are comfortable settling for living your life in a cycle, you are missing out on God's abundant life plan for you.

2. **Am I feeling stagnant, unable to move or accomplish anything?**

   Do you find yourself plowing day after day behind two oxen? The dust never goes away. The pointlessness of your job brings an attitude of worthlessness and frustration. Every day you wonder how to make it through until you get paid again. You can no longer remember the dreams you had for life. They are so distant, you cannot conjure up or reason why you ever imagined them. The desire in your heart to do and be someone different taps within your chest, wanting to be discovered, wanting to be uncovered. If you are feeling this way, you might be missing out on God's abundant life plan for you.

3. Am I going nowhere fast?

You are living a targetless, aimless, no directional lifestyle. Your definition of goals is something scored in soccer or hockey. Moving forward is something you only watch others do. The dreams you once had have been extinguished by the breath of others. Life has lost its zest. You are simply doing time. Words play in your head. Voices speak against you. The person you believed you could be is someone you do not recognize anymore. You have bought the lies of the enemy. You not only cannot remember what you desired to be, you no longer know how to desire to be anything but who you are told to be. If you are feeling this way, you might be missing out on God's abundant life plan for you.

4. Am I busy doing busyness?

Your calendar is filled with meetings, volunteering, social events, and work. While others believe your life is fulfilled, you fall short at every turn. Nothing seems to fit together. Minutes tick by leaving you wondering if this is all there will ever be to your life. You have an inability to say "no" to anything because that one more thing may be the one which gives you what you have been looking for in all the activities. You are people pleasing instead of seeking to please God. Frustration grows as your plate fills to the brim. You do a lot of things minimally. Your life is about putting out one fire after another, never looking back to see the damage the fire left. If you are feeling this way, you might be missing out on God's abundant life plan for you.

5. **Am I a person who lost my passion, stopped dreaming, can't see the future?**

No one wants to admit they have no passion for anything, or that they have stopped looking at the future in a hopeful, excited way. There are times in our lives when we feel stuck in a rut of nothingness rather than *enoughness*. Life is a process every single day. There are times that we face a state of staleness. Stale marriage. Stale parenting. Stale job. Mold is beginning to grow down the walls of our heart. We feel trapped and indecisive. Some of us start and stop one thing after another because we are searching to try and fill this exhausting tug of war within. All the self-help books tell readers to make goals, set a plan, see it through. There is this overwhelming feeling, knowing it isn't about setting a goal or keeping it, it is about making God's perfect will for our lives the goal.

In the Bible, I don't know if Elisha had a specific goal in mind. I can, however, imagine he didn't run to work every day shouting to the air, "I can't wait to drive those oxen again today! WooHoo!" Could there be anything less rewarding than walking behind two oxen's behinds all day? Maybe, while he was working every-day, he was planning for the moment when he stepped into God's purpose for His life. There was no hesitation when Elijah placed the cloak over him. The only way Elisha had the confidence to leave his job, burn his oxen, tell his family goodbye and follow Elijah was because he knew that in spite of his present grueling schedule, he was created to do something different - he just didn't know what it was.

Many of you may know the story of David - the one who killed the giant Goliath? As a Biblical story, it is probably the most popular. David, the youngest of the twelve sons of Jesse, kept and cared for his father's sheep. During this time, the nation of Israel is engaged in a war against the Philistine army, and David's brothers have gone to fight in this war. The Philistines have a giant named Goliath on their side. The Bible tells us Goliath was over nine feet tall. Every day he came to the front line of the Philistine Army and taunted the Israelites, mocking God, and challenging them to fight him. This went on for forty days. It went on so long because there was no one in the Israelite Army who was willing to fight him. They were all scared to death, *shaking in their boots,* afraid of him and did nothing to stop his rages.

You've probably heard it before, the taunting from Goliath, the one who looks you in the eye from your mirror in the morning shouting, "You think you can do what? I'd like to see that! Who do you think you are?" The Goliaths in our minds always end with that laugh which seals the deal in our hearts. We can't do it - never will do it.

The father of David, Jesse, sends the young boy to bring back news from the frontlines about his brothers. This is the part where I have to jump in, I mean, who would do that? Send his youngest boy into a war zone - but it was all part of the plan - God's plan. David heard Goliath yelling and screaming at the Israelites, cursing God, disclaiming all that is mighty about Him. Of course, followed by a deep, guttural, haunting laugh...and David volunteered to fight the giant.

Prior to this life changing moment, David was a shepherd boy. He tended to his father's flocks of sheep. Shepherds were with their sheep all the time. I'm sure there were many hours, minutes, seconds of the day just sitting and watching...sitting and watching...sitting and watching. Sound familiar? Remember Elisha plowing behind oxen, day-after-day, plowing, and plowing, and plowing. Scripture tells us that while tending to the sheep, David killed a lion and a bear. In my imagination, I can picture that he practiced with his slingshot a lot. I can just see it. Scouting out a tiny animal -and BAM! The rabbit hopping near the bush across the field - BAM! Target after target - BAM! BAM! BAM! Even his recreation was a part of his RE-CREATION of what God would call him to do.

> *"But David said to Saul, 'Your servant was tending his father's sheep. When a lion or a bear came and took a lamb from the flock, I went out after him and attacked him, and rescued it from his mouth; and when he rose up against me, I seized him by his beard and struck him and killed him. Your servant has killed both the lion and the bear; and this uncircumcised Philistine will be like one of them, since he has taunted the armies of the living God.'"*
> *1 Samuel 17:34-36*

While his job seemed mundane, unseen and unimportant, he remained connected to his loving God. When the time came for him to fulfill his purpose, he was ready to do so. Saul tries to give David his armour to wear but it is bulky and heavy. David can barely move much less fight a giant! Sometimes, people will step in and try to tell us how to do what God has asked us to do. God doesn't need them. Recognize this. When you are doing what God has purposed you to do, He will equip you with everything you need to do it. David takes stones in a nearby river; puts them in the slingshot; and BAM! TAKES THAT GIANT OUT! Unbeknownst to him, his recreation was actually preparation.

We are continually being preloaded for the moment when God throws the cloak on us or uses the stone to knock the giant out. For Elisha, the preloading was building a relationship with God; standing in obedience to His Word; listening for the moment he was called. For David, the preloading was practicing skills. Doing the best job possible until he was called to do the job God prepared for him to do. What can you do to bring to the surface the person you really are in the eyes of God?

1. Spend Time in Prayer.

It seems obvious, but how many of us have found ourselves too busy to actually do it? James 1:5 tells us, *"If any of you lacks wisdom, let him ask God, who gives generously to all without reproach, and it will be given him."* The simplest journey to knowing who we were created to be is not found in magazines, online, in culture or society, or in our dysfunctional families, it is found in the simplest of ways. We ask God, then wait for an answer. When we commune with God in prayer, we develop a deep relationship with Him that no one else can have. It is ours. My husband often says that God speaks to us through thoughts, ideas, situations but primarily His Word.

I lived in Chicago for half of my life . Winters can be a bit tough to say the least - especially for someone who grew-up in the South. In the South, if snow is even a remote possibility, everyone hurries to the grocery store to buy groceries and suddenly we have an impromptu day out of school. Cars are filled with gas. Flashlights, batteries, candles, bottled water become valuable commodities - for a snowflake flurry or 2 inches of snow that lasts MAYBE a day or two.

But in Chicago, winters are harsh; yet, people scurry around as if it is just another day. One winter in Chicago, we had the kind of snow storm that leaves every ounce of you cold - the kind of *nothing anyone can do about it* cold - and on top of that, we lost power in the early morning hours. I heard my daughter screaming out for me - "Mommy! I'm scared! Mommy!" The darkness over-whelmed me. I couldn't see my own hand in front of my face. I knew the way to her room. I'd made the trek a thousand times before, so I calmly called out her name. "I'm here baby! I'm coming!"

I knew her voice and she knew mine. When she heard me, she stopped crying. Why? Because we had a relationship. One in which we listened and talked to one another. One where we don't have to see each other to know who we are. See, my daughter didn't hear a stranger's voice - she heard my voice - she knew my voice - she trusted my voice. My daughter had heard my voice day-after-day-after-day-after-day. Recognition came instantly. It is no different with God. We learn His voice by spending time with Him, day-after-day-after-day-after-day.

2. Know His Word.

Having an experience of God's Word jumping off of the page into a personal experience and application into your life cannot be compared to only hearing someone else's explanation of His Word. The reality is, sometimes, we want someone else to tell us what we need to know instead of us learning it or having a personal moment of revelation ourselves. I will admit, I do not like reading directions. I look at the picture. Then, I just want someone to show me how it works so I can just do it - whatever *it* is. Recently, I had a message on my car dashboard that said, remote key battery is low, service is required. I thought to myself, I should be able to figure this out on my own. I passed the dealership that made the car and went to the battery section of the nearest store and started trying to do it myself. I ignored the manual written by the maker of the car. Well, by the process of elimination, of what batteries would not fit into the key shape, I got the battery needed after breaking the key a little in the process. With God's Word - you don't want to learn by the process of elimination and volunteer for extra moments of breaking. God has written His story for you. The manual is in hand, the dealer is on site. His message is very clear and specific for you. No one can tell you ALL of what God wants to tell you, because no one knows the message He has for you and your life.

Get out your manual(Bible) and start reading His Word. I always stress the importance of owning a Bible in the version and translation that you personally understand. Invest in a good Bible and set aside time to dive into it. There is nothing more important that you need to do. Learn what He says. Learn His promises. Learn to love Who He is.

3. Develop Your Gifts - Use Your Passions

What are you really good at doing almost effortlessly? I have a friend who can come into a room - her eyes move back and forth - her mind starts clicking - she starts moving furniture, organizing, and cleaning. She can turn chaos and complete disarray into order and structure. I love what she can do. It is so effortless for her. We've told her she needs to start her own company - that's how good she is.

I have another friend who can read, comprehend and strategize solutions faster than anyone I know. If there is such a thing as a computer brain, she has it. I often refer to her accurately as a genius. Not only is she a professor, but after practicing law at other firms, she now owns her own law firm with multiple locations.

Another friend of mine can plan and orchestrate details of an event in her sleep. She is the type who just sees the flow of time and function. I can almost hear her mind moving, working, shaping it into a functioning machine as she irons out the structure of how the event should work. She started her own event planning company and wrote a how-to manual in the process.

When I lived in the south, I knew of a lady who came to the US from another country. Because she was undocumented, it was difficult to work and make a living for herself and three children. Apparently, her grandmother was an amazing cook and taught her to cook authentic dishes. She went around to construction crews, offering lunch. Before long, she was filling orders for every day of the week. After a few months, she hired another lady to help her. Her business thrived. The beautiful part of the story was that she loved the Lord. With each lunch, she put encouraging scriptures, written in her first language. Not only did she share her passion, she shared her testimony as well. No matter how small an act might seem to be, it can have a huge impact.

What are your passions? Your strengths? Your gifts? How can you use those to tap into the person God purposed you to be? Your *yes* could be connected to others' blessings. The thing that you are supposed to do could not only bless you, but it could possibly employ, inspire and engage others on their own personal journeys. It is time to step into *His marvelous light and claim the excellencies of Him Who called you.*

HAD ENOUGH: LET'S TAKE IT PERSONAL

Have you ever ordered something at a restaurant you thought you wanted until you tasted it? Immediately, when you began to taste it, you thought ehhhhh, something's missing? You can't pinpoint exactly what. The dish you ordered looked better than it tasted. Some of our lives are like that. We wish for, want for, pray for and order certain things; however, when we get a taste of the reality of what we thought we wanted, we can sense that something is missing. The next action must be made with urgency. We must stop partaking and say, "I ordered or asked for the wrong thing." You must announce, I've HAD ENOUGH. If we don't make this decision with urgency, we can keep nibbling away at something that won't just nibble back, but it will devour us. The enemy is like a roaring lion seeking whom he may nibble at? No. Entertain? No. Tickle? No. Devour! Settling will eat away at the true you.

Settling for what's immediately in front of you versus stretching for what's ahead of you will lead you to a life of less than, when God has called you to greater than. I remember nearing the end of my undergraduate journey and being offered a radio job that was right there in front of me. There was nothing wrong with the job or the station, I just could feel that this role would be 'settling.' There was something more I was to do that was not exactly in my hand, but it was in my reach. I tasted ordinary during summer jobs and internships at various places, and I could distinguish that 'something' was missing. I didn't know all that was next, but I knew where I was, was not ALL I was supposed to be doing in that season. While working at my radio job in college, I didn't know that relocation, graduate school graduations, and full time ministry included the very music that I had been playing on the job, and it was all just ahead of me. But God did. Let Him order for you. He'll order your thoughts, order your steps, and order your stops.

Psalm 34:8 says, *"Oh taste and see that the Lord is Good. Taste and see! What God has for you won't leave you longing, it will leave you feeling your enoughness in Him as you experience and depend on His more than enoughness in every area of your life."*

Decide and declare it with me, I've HAD ENOUGH of the ordinary because I know that I HAVE ENOUGH of the extraordinary God in me to live out my ENOUGHNESS.

IN WHAT AREAS OF YOUR LIFE ARE YOU FEELING LIKE, EHHHH SOMETHING IS MISSING?

Examples:

Prayer Life

Relationship With My Sister Friends

List below as you pray and reflect:

ENOUGH IS ENOUGH

//

YOUR LINE IN THE SAND THAT PUTS AN END TO SELF DOUBT

> *"Yet you, Lord, are our Father. We are the clay, you are the potter; we are all the work of your hand."*
> Isaiah 64:8

So it is time...it is time to draw the line in the sand. There are always moments in life - moments which define us, make us who we are, good or bad. If you take a second, I am sure images of defining events, instrumental words, certain successes or failures come to your mind which you can unequivocally, without a shadow of doubt, say changed you, impacted you, hurt you, or encouraged you. And, I am certain, there is probably one or more of each that you can remember detail after detail. Most of these moments are not marked by a specific date or time. They dress themselves in hardship, tough decisions, or life battles, some of which we brought on ourselves and others that chose us. They show up in photographs or old home movies and the sounds and smells of the day are as memorable as the day it all happened.

These events create filters in which we view the people around us, our world, and who we are. Our reactions stem from perceived and unperceived attitudes which encourage or discourage us from doing one thing or another. Whether we call it baggage, anchors, ups and downs of life, or happenings, we all have them tucked away in places we can access or not access. Consciously or unconsciously, these life events demonstrate to us significance in who we are. Today, at this very moment, is one of those defining events for you - the day you draw the line in your sand. The day you look at yourself with the *ENOUGHNESS* of Jesus Christ.

I have always wanted to have testimonies of what God kept me from versus what God kept me through. However, God had a keeping plan beyond my plan. There have been many episodes in my life that He kept me through, These became not only defining moments, but they became refining moments.

We each have relationships on Earth, where when certain situations arise, it redefines the relationship. These journeys with God redefine the relationship and bring us closer to Him as our Keeper, Author, and Finisher of our faith.

One of those refining, redefining moments happened during my high school graduation week. After what I felt was a life of everyone cheering for me and celebrating my *Enoughness*, some of the narratives begin to change. I failed my honors English final, which I needed to pass in order to graduate with my class. I was crushed and embarrassed. First of all, everything seemed to always work out for me. That doesn't mean it was all easy, but I had never faced anything like this. As Co-Captain of the Cheer Squad and one of the Senior Student Council Leaders of the class, I couldn't begin to understand what not graduating with my classmates and friends looked like. To add insult to injury, I had a solo with the chorus that was singing during graduation! Try explaining that one away. I had been accepted into the colleges I had applied to and had won several pageant scholarships; yet, even with all these accomplishments, I still was not ENOUGH to graduate from high school with my class. All I could think about was what I was missing. Graduation was going to be so fun. We had practiced and lined up by last name. My best friend and I just so happened to be next to each other.

To some of you, this may not seem like a big deal, but, for my young seventeen-year-old mind, it was devastating - devastating in several ways. For one, I had never had anything rock my world in such a way before. Now, I do not profess to be perfect by any means; but, as I explained earlier, my mother was a rock. Our family unit stood firm. I can only wish for others to have what I had in my mom, grandmother, aunt and uncles. What may have been lacking in a fatherless family was multiplied by the support of others in my family. I reaped tremendous benefits from the way in which I was raised. As in any good story, a little rain not only must fall - it will fall.

Enter my High School Honors English Final Exam…

I did not pass it. Maybe it was senioritis. Maybe it was two feet in a future that hadn't begun because I needed to finish the past before I entered it. Maybe it was because I had that class first period when many activities meetings happened, and I missed the information I was supposed to be learning. It could have been my own extra-curricular busyness that I chose over studying that subject, but never had I failed in this way. Perhaps, it was a typical teenager, "I don't want to do-it-ism!"

I don't know, but I assure you, if I had a time machine, I'd go back and figure out how to pass that test! However, not passing that test set me up for bigger tests that I would have to pass.

During this process, months before I would leave my hometown for college, I began to hear 'not enough' statements in a way that I hadn't heard before. Statements like, "She was never smart." "She was this not that." You know how people are, and you've probably experienced the same thing. What floored me in this season was not what the kids my age were saying - I was shocked at negativity from adults. Even in what I perceived as a time of failure, my family was right there supporting me. My mom, best friend, and Aunt Liz created a graduation for me in her kitchen after summer school was completed. My other family members had cancelled their trips in light of my not graduating with my class. Although I was embarrassed, I felt supported and loved. My aunt, who was the superintendent of another school system at the time, offered for me to stay with her for the summer and complete my requirements in her district. A change of scenery is always a boost and the opportunity to spend time with my aunt, my uncle and cousins would have been fun. But, in this instance, I knew I couldn't go. I had to finish where I failed.

During this season, I was introduced to the experience of living with the extremes of competing voices: the naysayers who are vocalizing the aspects of not *enoughness* and the supportive tribe chanting the more than *enoughness*. Such opposition can be confusing, and the competing sounds tend to make one wonder which voices are actually correct and which ones are lies. And while others were having graduation parties and celebrations, I was studying a course I had already had, in the summer, with zero friends in class with me. While I was devastated, I saw God's Hand in my life - even then.

God is more concerned about our character than our comfort. He allows situations to occur to make us realize a few things, most importantly, that we need Him. Also, maybe life had been a bit too easy for me up until this point, and we all know, when life happens, it's not easy. Humility is a wonderful teacher in life, and I got a hefty dose of it that summer. Humility is often the product of unwelcomed humiliation. It was humbling to spend the summer in school with a group I would normally classify and categorize as the bad kids - that is until I was a part of the class!

When we have our own missteps off of the path He has chosen for us - when our navigational skills get us lost in a storm - when we find ourselves lacking what we know we have the ability to do - we need a *line in the sand.* And not just *any* line in the sand. A line that says, "I'm not doing it anymore. I'm not saying it anymore. I'm not being it anymore. I'm changing my direction and the level of effort I am exerting."

Peter was one of the disciples of Jesus Christ and my favorite at that. God used his steps and his missteps and got glory out of it all. Peter is the perfectly imperfect faith filled rebel. He was the son of Jonah and by trade, a fisherman. In fact, when Jesus called him to serve as His disciple, Peter was fishing. Known as Simon Peter, which in the Greek translation means 'rock', Peter was known as a married man who lived in Capernaum.

His passion was unmatched by any of the other disciples. Overrun with enthusiasm, Peter reacted before his brain had time to make a complete thought at times. Any of you like that or know someone who is always reacting without a moment's hesitation? Full of zealousness and boldness, Peter seemed to have more energy and creativity than he knew how to control. In two different scenarios, the Bible tells us, Peter jumped out of a boat, fully clothed into the water. One such time was in a terrible storm in order to walk on the water to Jesus. The other time, he was less than 100 yards from shore. It makes me laugh to think about Peter running through the water while the other disciples stayed dry just rowing passed him in the boat.

He made a practice of challenging and questioning Jesus. Peter was the guy in the room who said what everyone else was thinking but didn't have the courage to say.

"Jesus, how many times do we have to forgive someone?"

"Are there rewards for following Jesus?"

He was the first to declare Jesus as the Son of the Living God; yet, he denied Christ three different times when He was arrested.

Peter reminds me of one of those crazy, bouncy rubber balls. The ones that are so hard to catch? You know the ones! We all know a 'Peter' type or have been a 'Peter' type in certain scenarios. Quick responses were synonymous with Peter. He loved to question, and he loved to answer. He created problems but offered solutions. He was quick to answer and just as quick to challenge. Peter wanted options but he also wanted decisions. Most of the time, Peter was fully unleashed, wide-open, exercising little to no restraint.

And then he drew *the line in the sand.*

The first time Peter began drawing his line in the sand was the first time he lept into the water after Jesus. This story appears in three of the four Gospels. Only in one of the accounts, however, do we learn that Peter got out of the boat. Early in the day, the disciples had witnessed Jesus feeding 5000 people with five loaves of bread and two fish. Jesus sent the disciples ahead of Him, and He went up on the mountain to pray. The disciples encountered a fierce storm which they battled most of the night. Even more terrifying than the storm is what they believed to be a ghost walking on the water. It is in Matthew that we learn Peter called out to this ghost.

Matthew 14:28 - 33, "'*Lord, if it's you,' Peter replied, 'tell me to come to you on the water.' 'Come,' he said. Then Peter got down out of the boat, walked on the water and came toward Jesus. But when he saw the wind, he was afraid and, beginning to sink, cried out, 'Lord, save me!' Immediately, Jesus reached out His hand and caught him. 'You of little faith,' He said, 'why did you doubt?' And when they climbed into the boat, the wind died down. Then those who were in the boat worshiped Him, saying, 'Truly, you are the Son of God.'*"

"*Then Peter got down out of the boat…*" Peter took that first step - the step where faith comes in. Faith can be confusing because there are things we can have faith in that do not come to fruition. Look at Peter. He stepped out in faith, believing in the supernatural power of God when Jesus called him out onto the water. His action speaks volumes to me because when Jesus called him, Peter acted. I would've liked the story better if Peter had walked all the way to Jesus, or would I have? The beauty of Peter stepping out is when Jesus calls us to do something, it may not always work out as we expected; however, no matter how it ends, God is there. Whether the fear of the storm overcame him or he doubted his ability to do it, Peter takes his eyes off Jesus and sinks into the water. My favorite word in the verse is the word *immediately.*

"*Immediately Jesus reached out His hand and caught him.*"

There is such confidence in that word. It tells us that Jesus is our safety net - always watching - always available - always willing to catch us. There is an underlying message in this as well. Sometimes, God may call us to do something that doesn't work out the way we thought. When we look at the verse closely, it is Peter who suggests that he walk out onto the water to Jesus. I don't know why Jesus didn't say, "It is me, Peter, but you need to stay in the boat." He could have said that. The whole stepping out on the water was actually Peter's idea; however, Jesus called Peter out of the boat. And in so doing, He knew what would happen. He also knew He would save Peter from the storm. Jesus saved Peter from his own doubt on location.

What happened in the water was more about developing Peter's character than walking on the water. Sound familiar? Haven't we all had those experiences? Maybe you are going through something right now which God is working on your character rather than your answer. Comfort is what we are seeking - completeness is what God is seeking.

History suggests that several years after the Resurrection of Jesus, Mark was a disciple of Peter. Scholars believe that Mark wrote the Book of Mark according to what Peter told him about the life of Christ. In Mark's account of the story, there is no mention of Peter walking on the water. Why would Mark leave it out? My guess is, Peter didn't tell him. He left that part of the story out. Something that was once so significant to Peter, he failed to mention to Mark. Peter had changed. He had developed into the Evangelist Jesus needed him to be and his attempt to walk on the water was no longer relevant. His thoughts were not on himself anymore but on Jesus.

Ahhhhh...could it be, when we wrap ourselves in the narrative blanket, the one which tells us who we are to the world - how we do not measure up - what we are capable of doing and what we are not capable of doing - it is because we have taken our eyes off Jesus and focused them on ourselves? As we unfold our potential, we need to be assured our eyes are on the person God knows we are - not the person we created in our minds to be. Jesus called Peter out onto the water because He knew the person He created Peter to be. Peter was still holding on to the person Peter believed himself to be. That is the doubt Jesus is talking about. Peter doubted the person Jesus knew him to be.

I wonder how often God whispers in our ears - you can do this! It is all in your DNA. D.N.A.= Do Not Abandon God's Truth! Don't doubt My Handiwork. I wonder how many times we turn our heads because all the voices around us - like the storm - keep us from recognizing and hearing what God is saying. Like Peter, we fail to realize we are enough in Jesus Christ to walk on water; to get into that college; to lose weight; to start a new career; to adopt that little boy; to be debt free; to get married; to buy that house; to write that book; to sing that song; to _____ (you fill in this blank).

For Peter the final line in the sand, the one which launched his ministry probably came on the beach, (an actual site for a line in the sand), when he spotted Jesus walking on the shore. The story comes from John 21. It is after the Resurrection of Christ. Peter, Thomas, Nathanael, and two other disciples were fishing. Jesus yells to them from the shore, "Friends, haven't you any fish?"

When they respond, "No!" He tells them to cast their net on the right side of the boat. It becomes so full of fish that they cannot bring it into the boat.

> " ⁷ *Then the disciple whom Jesus loved (John) said to Peter, "It is the Lord!" As soon as Simon Peter heard him say, "It is the Lord," he wrapped his outer garment around him (for he had taken it off) and jumped into the water.* ⁸ *The other disciples followed in the boat, towing the net full of fish, for they were not far from shore, about a hundred yards.* ₉ *When they landed, they saw a fire of burning coals there with fish on it, and some bread."*
> John 2:7-9

I love that Peter jumped into the water. His heart was full of love for Jesus. He couldn't get closer fast enough. I have a friend whose son would say the cutest thing when he was a toddler. He would crawl into her lap, wrap his arms around her neck and whisper, "Closer! Closer, Mommy!" Sometimes we cannot get close enough to the ones we love. Peter could not get close enough, fast enough. It is this kind of thirst which brings us to where we need to be. When our heart longs for God's Word; desires to be near Him; seeks His answers, we are primed to find the *ENOUGHNESS* He has for us.

When the disciples reached the shore, their net overflowing with fish, Jesus asked them to bring Him some fish to cook over the fire. When they finished eating, Jesus asked Peter:

"*Simon, son of John, do you love me more than these?'*

'Yes, Lord,' he said, 'you know that I love you.'

Jesus said, 'Feed my lambs.'

Again Jesus said, 'Simon, son of John, do you love me?'

He answered, 'Yes, Lord, you know that I love you.'

Jesus said, 'Take care of my sheep.'

The third time he said to him, 'Simon, son of John, do you love me?'

Peter was hurt because Jesus asked him for the third time, 'Do you love me?' He

said, Lord, you know all things; you know that I love you.'

Jesus said, 'Feed my sheep.'"

It was Peter's defining moment. It was Peter's line in the sand. I am constantly amazed at what God can do when we submit ourselves to Him and walk in the purpose He designed for us. If Peter can come to grips with the person he was created to be, there is hope for you and me. I used to be confused by this, wondering what Jesus meant by asking Peter three times, "Do you love me?" Was He passively reprimanding Peter about the denials the night He was arrested? Was He covering different areas of love and different ways to love people?

There are many ideas and explanations for this conversation between Peter and Jesus. I think Jesus was trying to give Peter a key to his identity in Christ. Do you love me? then, FEED MY SHEEP. He was commissioning Peter to be a shepherd. Not just any shepherd, a shepherd of Jesus' flock. The world we live in is a world of power and control. The person who holds the power - holds the control. Peter tried to conform to the world. He tried to make Jesus conform to the world. We see this many times with Peter's interactions. The best example was in the garden the night of Jesus' arrest. Peter either did not understand this was the plan, or he wanted to set the outcome. In John 18:10 we learn that when the soldiers came to arrest Jesus, *"Simon Peter, who had a sword, drew it and struck the high priest's servant, cutting off his right ear. (The servant's name was Malchus)."*

A fighter, a loyal servant, a man of action, Peter was ready for battle. He would take on the world for the Kingdom of Jesus Christ. His interpretation of what was happening and Jesus' were different. Peter couldn't see the bigger picture and probably when Jesus reprimands him and puts the ear back on Malchus, Peter's confusion spirals out of control.

We do the same - jump into the middle of what God is doing to implement our own plan. Afterall, don't we know better than anyone else how our lives should look? Having seen Jesus perform many amazing miracles, Peter had no doubt they had the power to take control of the soldiers and claim the throne. How often had he heard Jesus was the King - it was His Kingdom - finally, they'd be rid of the Romans and oppression? Why not make it happen? Why not force the anticipated result?

Jesus is telling Peter, "Find your identity in me. Do you love me, Peter? Then, feed my sheep."

When we fall in love with Jesus Christ...when He holds our heart...when we love as He loves...we have the heart we need to become the person He created us to be. Matthew 22:37 says, *"Love the Lord your God with all your heart and with all your soul and with all your mind."* In Him, we are *enough*. And *enough* is just that... *enough*.

Falling in love with Jesus Christ is not a feeling. It is a commitment. A commitment that does not change with situations or circumstances. Deep within us, we must reflect a loyalty and faithfulness to weather any storm, any obstacle, any deception, any fear. We have to recognize Romans 8:31, *"...If God is for us, who can be against us?"* This love is limitless, unconditional, unbroken. This love comes when we dig deep, connect, and devote *who* we are to God.

Are you ready to commit? Is it time to recognize that *Enough is Enough*? You are *enough* in Him. Being *enough* in Jesus Christ is *enough*. Acts 17:28 says, *"For in Him we live and move and have our being."* John 15:4 says, *"Abide in me, as I abide in you."*

The question however is what does that look like? There was a television game show that my grandmother used to watch called, *To Tell The Truth*. By the time I was old enough to understand it, we were watching reruns. However, it was fun to watch my grandma trying to guess along with the celebrity panel who the real person was. The panelist (celebrities) question a group of 3 people all claiming to be a particular person - an Olympic gymnast or the inventor of aluminum foil. Just a few years ago, I realized the show was still in syndication. My favorite part of the show was when the spotlight would flash around and the announcer would say, "Would the REAL (name of person) please STAND UP!" Of course, the objective was to confuse the panelist as to who the real person was.

Very similarly, we try to be all types of people, none of whom are the real you and me. We can have moments of having chameleon characteristics, blending in with whoever and whatever is around us. Lovingly, God works to redirect us, refocus us, and restore us to the person He needs us to be. He knows everything about us, and He knows how He has equipped us. The key is bringing the person within us out into the open. Let's start by realizing we are uniquely and beautifully made. In understanding this, our hearts must reflect the love of Jesus Christ. I hear Him whisper, "Do you love me, Tara? Feed my sheep. Do you love me, Tara? Feed my sheep. Do you love me, Tara? Then, feed my sheep." We are made to worship our Lord and disciple His people. This moment of realization put Peter on the path to who he was predestined to be. It will do the same for you.

Over the next few weeks, consciously commit to a deeper relationship with Jesus Christ. One which begins the day in His Word and ends in His Word. One which recognizes the uniqueness of who you are in Jesus Christ. One which opens your heart to the freedom that can only come from loving Him. When those labels pop in your head, voice out loud, "I love you, Jesus. I am *enough* in you. And *enough* is *enough* to do and be who You created me to be."

It is time to start listening to the voice of God within us and not the voice of the world's demands of us. It is time to be intentional about the decisions we make on a daily basis - do they line up with the Word of God? Are they in line with the desires God has placed in our hearts?

One of the ways I used to help my children make a choice as to what they wanted to do, I helped them eliminate what they did not want to do. While it was a fun exercise for them, it was also an exercise in wisdom. We'd write out a list of options on pieces of paper and line them up across the table. I would ask, "What is a no choice? What on this list do you enjoy the least?" One by one, they would narrow it down to about three things. Then we would discuss the positive and negatives of each remaining choice until it was easy to determine what they truly wanted to do. While the first step toward finding our *enoughness* in Jesus Christ is connecting our hearts with His, the second step is eliminating the labels attached to us that are not us or that we no longer want to carry. As you develop your relationship with Jesus at a deeper level, I want you to begin to tear away the labels which do not belong to you or which you no longer want to carry. Peel them away in your mind. Actively decide you are no longer that person.

1. **Find Validation in Jesus** - Many of us need praise from others. It is one of the main reasons we are where we are, living a life which isn't ours but the world's. Accept that you can no longer rely on the satisfaction you get when you do exactly what others want you to do. Determine today - now - you are going to withdraw from having performance relationships. It is OK if someone isn't happy with you. As an adult, you can make decisions regarding your life. You do not need someone else's validation - only Christ's.

2. **Stop being who you aren't.** As your heart becomes closer to His, it will become more evident who you are in Jesus Christ and who you are not. There will be people who will try and entice you back as you leave the roles the world has made for you. It can be difficult, but admit and commit to the fact that some of those people need to be cut out of your life. Evaluate your list. Believe in who you are and know who you are not. Trust you have what it takes to become who you are in Christ.

3. **Love yourself.** There are days when we may have to tell ourselves repeatedly, "I love you. I love who you are. I love who you are becoming." There are days when we have to speak words of affirmation to ourselves more often. The most important conversations we have are the conversations we have with God and the ongoing conversations we have with ourselves. Try saying these words. "I am striving to be who God created me to be, and I love the person I am in Jesus Christ." Loving yourself as you are, as you were created to be, is a gift from God. It can only start with you.

Have you ever tried to wear shoes that don't fit? When I was in college, a friend of mine had the most gorgeous stilettos - a perfect match for the dress I was wearing to an event I'd been invited to attend. The problem was, they were ½ a size too small. But, they were too cute not to wear, right? Wrong! Thirty minutes into the evening and a few trips on the dance floor and my feet were screaming loud and clear! These shoes DO NOT FIT! Nothing ruins an evening more than feet that ache. Have you ever had a pain that changed your personality? A pain that changed how you would normally act or react to others? A pain that altered who you were as a person?

Well, all of those roles you are trying to squeeze into - those labels you are accepting as true when they couldn't be anything but - those negative, hurtful, mantras you play over and over in your head - are like the shoes I tried to wear that night. TAKE them off! God has the perfect size for you. He had a special fitting for you before you were born and your role He designed says that you are BIG enough - SMART enough - TALL enough - CUTE enough - FAST enough - SMALL enough - DARK enough - LIGHT enough - HEALED enough - REDEEMED enough - LOVED enough.

Why wear shoes that hurt your feet? Why wear a design that isn't right for you when there is one uniquely, perfectly, divinely made just for you? There's a Cinderella-sized shoe fit for you, a walk, a role for you to walk in that only fits YOU! A customized, tailor made fit for you that looks like and fits like nothing else, and it fits no one else.

ENOUGH IS ENOUGH: LET'S TAKE IT PERSONAL

When is enough enough?

I am admittedly an over accessorizer. I remember growing up going to the mall and seeing someone we knew from church every week who worked in cosmetics. While my mom and aunt were chatting it up with her, I was looking at Mrs. Sarah's hands noticing that she had a ring on every finger. I thought to myself, I couldn't wait to do that. Every birthday and holiday, I would ask for another accessory to achieve this goal. Then, I couldn't wait to wear big earrings. For my sweet sixteen, I had a big party, and my favorite gift request was big earrings. To this day, one of my favorite gifts to receive are nice big hoop earrings. However, although I liked big accessories, I often found myself in many settings where I would have to take them off.

I've always danced. From ages 3 -18 in ballet, tap and jazz at Pat Brown's School of Dancing to dancing through college on Clark Atlanta University's Dance Team then the School Gospel Choir's Praise Dance Ministry to starting the dance ministry at Fellowship Missionary Baptist Church, teaching choreography in various settings, and Zumba. In these dance settings, I would have to take all of these accessories off because of the potential dangers that wearing them could cause during movement. Throughout my adulthood, even in speaking settings, when getting mic'd up to speak, audio ministries would have to pull me to the side and say, please remove your earrings, we are hearing sounds from your jewelry and cannot clearly hear your words. My husband would often joke with me and say pick one accessory to take off. He would say, "I'm not sure that you need all the brooches, bracelets, necklaces, belts, earrings and rings on at the same time." I would laugh, taking something off while still enjoying the loudness of it all.

Sometimes in life, we are focused on the accessories of life. The external decorations and noises which can, not only distract us from the assignment we are to do but can also entangle us and cause us to focus on something that should not be the focal point.

What do you need to take off that's become a noisy accessory in your life?

When God says Enough - it's enough. No matter what the varying voices around you are saying, you have what you need in you to face what's before you.

God is saying, "You are enough because I am WITH you! I created you!"

You are not an incomplete creation, but God is saying that I am working through you as long as you live on this earth.

Philippians 1:6 says. "Being confident of this, that He who began a good work in you will carry it on to completion until the day of Christ Jesus."

When we esteem others' approval higher than God's pre-approval, we make the noisy, clanky, clamoring accessories of the opinions of others idols in our lives. Your Divine purpose from Heaven does not require co-signatures on Earth!

What do you need to take off that's become a noisy accessory in your life? _____

_____

_____

_____

Have you been missing the assignment for this season of your life while shopping for the accessory of acceptance? Perhaps you want to be accepted into a certain social circle, family clique, sorority/fraternity, social media status, board position, promotion, friend group, neighborhood.

What accessory have you been seeking? _____

_____

_____

In what ways have you focused on decorative accessories versus Divine assignments? _____

_____

_____

_____

In what ways do we focus on things that aren't the main purpose of our lives in God's perspective? _____

_____

_____

Have you been shopping and searching for the accessory of approval? _____

_____

_____

_____

In what ways have you been seeking the accessory of attention and appreciation?
In some roles, you may not receive the appreciation you believe that you deserve.
Know that God sees the heart of the matter whether you get the public apprecia-
tion or not._____

_____

_____

_____

JUST ENOUGH

YOUR DEFICIENCIES THAT GLORIFY GOD'S SUFFICIENCY

> *"Not that we are competent in ourselves to claim anything for ourselves, but our competence comes from God."*
> 2 Corinthians 3:5

I remember being a teenager the first time I saw her. I noticed her bright red fingers before anything else. She was fashionable. Her hair was styled like someone on television, and she was meticulous in dress from her accessories to her shoes. Even the way she sat with my mom, her back straight, her legs crossed, her head tilted slightly to the side, listening to my mother's story, she gleaned with perfection. I thought to myself, "That's how I'm going to be when I grow up." I desperately wanted to know what my Mama and her were talking about but when I got too close, my mom would tell me to go to another room for a little while. I watched from around the corner of our home when the woman left our house that day. Her car was expensive and as she opened the door to get in and leave, she noticed me. I waved at her – she only smiled – a sad smile – one with little expression.

Several weeks later, I heard my mom talking about the lady to my aunt. Sadly, she had thought about taking her own life. My aunt told me the lady had made many wrong choices in life and was struggling to live with those choices. At that time, it didn't seem possible to me that someone so put together, so immaculate on the outside, could be struggling so much on the inside.

When I saw her again, she looked the same, but I realized something I still consider today. The gift under the brightly lit tree may have the shiniest paper, a bow perfectly tied and holding it all together, but all of it has no significance if the inside is empty.

I often think of those overloaded piles of gifts that some of us give to our kids on Christmas. After all of the investment and time spent on giving the gifts, often children are more excited about the wrapping and the box than it's contents. Picture this. Your child is ignoring the gift that was in the box, but chooses to give all of the attention to and spend all of their time, playing with the box! Do we treat God in a similar way? After all of the investment and time he spent on us, giving us the gifts He's given to us, we get more excited about the wrapping than our own internal content. Are we enamored with playing with the box, while ignoring the gifts in us?

Do we spend more time on our hair than renewing our minds? Do we spend more time on our clothing than guarding our hearts? Do we spend more time on our skin regimen than our word regimen? Many of us spend a lot of time making sure our outsides look picture perfect for the world. We post stories on Instagram and wait for validation. How many likes are there? We review our comments on Facebook. What did she mean by that comment? Why did she say it like that? We seek validation from the outside because it makes us believe in our acceptance by the world. The number of followers – the number of friends – all give us a barometric reading of how we are measuring up. We dress to please. We post to please. We change our hair according to trends. We drive cars we can't afford. Purchase bags that are worth more than we have because of their name brands despite the costs. Our behavior reflects what others want and not necessarily what God asks.

Maybe we indulge in certain things in order to fit in, not because we even have an appetite for that particular thing. Maybe we put other people down in order to get the attention of others and make ourselves appear better than we believe we actually are. Maybe we lie about ourselves to stand out more or catch someone's eye.

There's a term known as 'catfishing.' Catfishing is when someone uses a fake identity online to foster a relationship, albeit based in deception. The imaging is different than the reality. Could we be 'catfishing' - looking like someone we actually are not. All of these actions point to the thirst for validation.

Where does your validation come from?

Jesus tells a story of a man with two sons. It comes from Luke 15:11-32 and is known as "The Story of the Prodigal Son." The younger son, who by birthright would receive 1/3 of his father's inheritance, comes to his dad and asks for his portion of wealth. Luke 15:12 tells us, *"The younger one said to his father, 'Father, give me my share of the estate.' So, he divided his property between them."*

It is not often addressed, but the verse says "them." It doesn't say "him." It doesn't say, "The father gave the younger boy his 1/3 of the estate but told the older son he would need to wait until the father had died. The scripture indicates that the father, at the younger son's request, divides the estate between them. THEM. Older brother – younger brother. And, it does not specify amounts, although historically, the older son normally received 2/3's of the father's wealth and the younger son 1/3.

As we read further, we learn shortly after his father gives him the money, the younger son takes off to a distant land and squanders the money on wild living. Now, we can only imagine what is meant by "wild living," but I can tell you, while he had the money, the younger son probably had a lot of friends. Friends who hung around for the drinks, the dinners, the dances, the perks of living alongside a young, crazy, fun guy who has a lot of money. I bet he had the best clothes, the prettiest girls, the LIKES, and followers online. I bet when his stories posted, his numbers online skyrocketed. I'm sure that everything he wanted and anyone that he wanted was in his reach. He might have even been thinking back to his father and brother's life and laughing. He believed that he was at the pinnacle of success. He was trending. Life couldn't get any better than it is now.

And as everything in the world is...it was temporary. The fun rise had an imminent fall.

> Luke 15:14-16 continues, "After he had spent everything, there was a severe famine in that whole country, and he began to be in need. So, he went and hired himself out to a citizen of that country, who sent him to his fields to feed pigs. He longed to fill his stomach with the pods that the pigs were eating, but no one gave him anything."

At this point, the younger son's worth had been contingent upon money, friends, materialism, and worldly acceptance. However, when he *"began to be in need,"* where were these friends? These friends who liked his Instagram stories and enjoyed the drinks and appetizers on his dime? Did anyone offer a place for him to stay? Bring him a meal? Loan him some money? Do we know if he even asked for help from anyone? The answer to these questions is NO, because we really do not know. The reason behind the NO could be because of the shallowness of the friends, but also because when we base everything on the reaction and actions of others (the outside world), our insides bank on the outside. Like the package under the tree, we are left with nothing but emptiness because we based it all on appearances. I often tell my children, if Satan appeared as he really looked, no one would be interested in anything he had to say. Deception, whether by someone else or by ourselves, leads us to an empty dwelling place. The younger son finds himself longing for the food pigs are eating.

Some of us find ourselves in a similar situation. Not necessarily in the context of swine, but unrealistically viewing our lives in such a way, devaluing who we are, adapting to new norms within pig pens, not seeing ourselves as even worthy of having more. The younger son thinks back on his father, his brother, and the servants. *"When he came to his senses, he said, 'How many of my father's hired servants have food to spare, and here I am starving to death! I will set out and go back to my father and say to him: Father, I have sinned against Heaven and against you. I am no longer worthy to be called your son; make me like one of your hired servants.' So, he got up and went to his father."* - Luke 15:17-20.

I love the first few words of this verse, *"When he came to his senses..."* Yes!

Lord, help us to come to our senses. Another transliteration of this same passage says, "When he came to himself!" Lord, help us to see who we really are. Help us to come to ourselves! Help us to stop longing for the "*pods that the pigs are eating*" and start longing for what You have for us. Right now, you are probably thinking, who longs for pods that the pigs are eating? NOT ME! When we settle for less, when we were ordained for more, we're longing for the pig slop! Instead of the best our Heavenly Father has planned for us, everything we often long for is less. Sometimes we even pray for God to help us make our "less than" plans work.

The state of mind of the son is significant here as well. He believed because of his actions; because of his mistakes; because of the sequence of events which led him to the place he was in, he was no longer worthy to be called a *son*. He was ready to settle for *servant*. It is easy to come to this place whether you realize it or not. There are times we, like the Prodigal Son, think we know better about our future than God does. The younger son had big dreams. He was going to conquer the world - but on his terms - his way - and his father allowed him to do so for a certain amount of time.

It might not have been the first time the father had heard this idea from the younger son. This could have possibly been a repeat request. I could imagine, the father talking to the boy about the importance of money; how to find true success; how to be wise with our money and save; how patience is a virtue; and how to work hard for what you have. This final request was just what dad needed to say - "Time to learn a valuable life lesson."

Many of us find ourselves in a similar pattern. Maybe we haven't been wise with our choices. Perhaps we were determined to do the wrong thing. Maybe we haven't listened to or followed a Godly plan for all of our lives. Maybe through a series of events, none of which we had a choice in the matter, we are left wanting and in need. The rejection of the world, the labels which incorrectly identify us, the search for validation in the world, lead us to a place of emptiness and insecurity. We devalue or dismiss our possibilities in God because somewhere deep down, we do not believe we are worthy of them.

The younger son determines that he is heading home. Can you just imagine his frame of mind? Whatever concerned him about his return, he had resolved himself to believe, his place was with his father - however that looked. As he turns the corner for his home, his father sees him coming from a distance. For me, this is the most beautiful part of the story. The Bible tells us, *"But while he was still a long way off, his father saw him and was filled with compassion for him; he ran to his son, threw his arms around him and kissed him."* This tells me his dad was always keeping a watchful eye out for him. He never stopped looking or expecting his return. The father does not wait until the son gets to him. He doesn't wait to see what the son might say or not say – the minute he catches a glimpse of him, he RUNS to him, throws his arms around him, and kisses him. The father tells the servants to kill the fattened calf and prepare a feast to celebrate the return of his son.

I wish there was a follow-up story. I would really love to know more details of what happened next. We are left with only our imaginations, but we can assume a few things: 1) He learned where to seek validation. 2) He learned the value of a true relationship. 3) He learned who he was to his father, unconditionally!.

It is very easy to fall into the trap of seeking validation. Who we are…What we have…Who we know…How they see us…are no indicator of the person we are.

The problem with seeking our security in an external environment is eventually, we won't find it. Our mindset is fixed on the addictive, need-to-know, approval of people. The never-enough accolades of others will come to an end, even an abrupt halt at times, leaving us as empty as the beautifully wrapped Christmas present under the tree – insignificant and worthless. Setbacks easily paralyze the external validator, leaving her fearful of failure and with little to no confidence. Lack of confidence leads to a lack of self-worth and hopelessness. Before long, we find ourselves like the Prodigal Son, longing for pods of pigs.

As we determine who we aren't according to the world, we also need to look at who we want to be according to the word!. In the Prodigal Son, the younger son wanted to be "that" guy – the one with the money, the fancy car, the women. He wanted to be the one people are talking about, people wish to be, and want to follow. The problem is, it isn't the person people talk about or wish to be or want to follow, it is the "stuff" they are after. A huge part of being who we are created to be is knowing who we aren't, and always doing away with seeking a false perspective of ourselves in a way that does not honor God.

I knew a particular lady who would always answer the question, "How are you?" with the statement, "I am blessed and highly favored." While it sounds wonderful, her appearance seemed anything but favored. She had a debilitating disease which left her with crippled hands and in a wheelchair. My understanding was that her body constantly hurt from the chronic pain and because the disease was so rare, there was little the medical community could do to help her. She didn't have any children or living siblings; there essentially was no one in her life who could care for her. With no financial support or physical support, she found himself in a state-run facility –still saying, "I'm blessed and highly favored."

We feel blessed and favored in the Lord despite our circumstances when our needs are met in Him. All that we are. Everything we go through. Choices we make good or bad, all come around to a simple truth – there is no circumstance, no consequence, no problem or issue that God will not use to grow us, to use us, to advance His call on our lives.

> *Paul writes in Philippians 4:12, "I know what it is to be in need, and I know what it is to have plenty. I have learned the secret of being content in any and every situation, whether well fed or hungry, whether living in plenty or in want."*

The secret to finding our direction and purpose in the Lord, "our *enoughness*," is our ability to recognize the circumstances we face today are tools for God to use to strengthen us as we walk according to His wishes and His plans. As a mom, wife, and ministry leader, there have been times in my life when I felt tugged and pulled in multiple directions at the same time all the time. Paying bills, what each person will and won't eat, who needs to be where by what time, travel schedules, repairs, what did I forget? You name it – my name was on it. Feeling this way tells me, all of these things are dependent upon me – on my ability to do a good job – on my skills – on my efforts – on my…my…my. If this is the case, failure is going to result no matter how good or bad I am. None of this is on me. Without His provision and direction, I might last a little while. You may thrive a few years, but eventually, the realities of the world and our weak selves' surface.

It is not God's intent for us to live under the pressures of everything depending on us. It is not His purpose for our lives to be filled with shallow dreams and desires to be recognized for material wealth or worldly status. It is not the desire of God for us to see ourselves as anything but His. When we lean on Him, rely on Him, look to Him, and focus on Him, we will experience the *enoughness* of Him. "When I am weak, that's when I am made strong!" -2 Corinthians 12:2. As believers in Jesus Christ, we have to start with an intentional act to accept who we are in Him, today. Start by being today's best. That is the best you can be today.

Most of us spend our lives in an if-then cycle. We are waiting for that moment we lose 20 pounds, then we will be who we are. If we buy that house in this neighborhood, we will be where we need to be. That car, that career, that baby, that relationship - if we can get there, then… All of those wishes could come true, and guess what? You will still be searching because you have not learned to love who you are - who God created you to be - right here - right now. Stop blaming who you aren't and start seeing who you are. Self-acceptance starts on your knees. It starts with a prayer of thankfulness for the person God created you to be. That doesn't mean you can't reach to higher levels to become more educated or change jobs or lose weight; what it means is being intentional to love who you are - right here - right now. As you step out to improve yourself, it won't be anything but simply that - an improvement. As a parent, I have watched my children grow, develop, and learn so many things. I do not love them any more because they are potty trained or can ride a bike. I am not happier in my relationship as a mother to them because they can add and subtract. Just because they improved, doesn't make me any different towards them. I loved them in diapers, and I loved them out of diapers. Keep that mindset about yourself.

Society spends a lot of time talking about judgment. It talks very little about how we view ourselves and judge ourselves unfairly. Take your arms and wrap them across your chest. Give yourself a much needed hug. Get used to doing this, because you are going to do it every day. Why? Because you love who you are. When we love someone, we hug them. We celebrate them. We accept them just the way they are. I want you to make it a practice to give yourself a much needed hug every day.

Resolve yourself to accept who you are, where you have been, what you have done, and why you are different. Regret weighs heavy. Don't let it consume you or interfere with who you are and how you feel about yourself. Past mistakes are where they belong - in the past. So, let's start with *Who you are*...Remember that question? Let's start there. As you read these words, I want you to say it out loud, "I am exactly who I need to be right now. I am loved in a way I never knew could be possible by God, my Creator. I am capable of doing incredible, amazing things through Him because I am *enough* just as I am. "

Do you remember the old hymn *Just As I Am?* It is one of my favorites because it speaks to us in a way that is personal. God wants you just as you are. You don't need a shower. You don't need a better job. You don't need to go back to school. You don't have to be free of the addiction. You don't need to lose weight. The Hymn was written in 1834 by a woman named Charlotte Elliott who suffered from a debilitating illness. Her story is an incredible glimpse of how God can use us, no matter our condition. *Just As I Am* was written on a day when Charlotte was overcome with depression and sadness due to her illness. She reflected that in order to come to Jesus there is no standard of goodness. People are just enough. The third verse of her hymn reads, "Just as I am, though tossed about with many a conflict, many a doubt, fightings and fears within, without, O Lamb of God, I come, I come."

When we realize the truth that our best possible self is wrapped up in God, things change. We are no longer trying to find who we are in this temporal and temperamental world. We no longer are basing our happiness on what society tells us is the definition of success. Truthfully, there may be some dreams we need to tell "goodbye," and there may be some dreams we need to have the courage to act upon and have an actionable plan to do so. Success is defined in many ways, depending upon who you are allowing to define the word "success." Some define success by a dollar amount, a certain degree level, or a certain amount of possessions. Others define success as a certain marital status, a predetermined kid count or even by the lack of desire for either of the aforementioned. However the word 'success' has been defined in your context, you may have to take the time to detox and deprogram those thoughts if they are not aligned with the way you believe God is leading your life. Redefining success could be the beginning of you realizing your *enoughness*. By embracing a new meaning for success, you let go of the finish lines and gold stars that are attached to others' goals for you. Success can be redefined as being in God's perfect will for your life in this season of your life. Therefore, what success looks like for you could be distinctly different than what success looks like for me.

We must also recognize that our *enoughness* is not attached to some non-existent ideal. Feeling your own *enoughness* does not come from looking like someone you are not, sounding like someone else, or pretending to have a gift you don't have. If you spend your life trying to be "them," then who is going to be you? This planet needs you!

Undoubtedly, it takes work to deprogram the ideals that have been put in front of us for years; but, we have to dig until we get to our true core. I once heard someone say, "God may ask you to move a mountain. Do not doubt that He will equip you to move it - but that equipment may be a shovel." This statement has always scared me a little bit. We want to think if God equips us, it will be easy. Nothing could be further from the truth. Sometimes, the process with God is anything but easy. What we have to have is the willingness to do it - to do what He asks us to do - to pick up that shovel and start digging deep.

Take a moment and allow your best self to step out and have a little chat with you. Sound a bit strange? The reality of this exercise is you need to know that within you is the person God created you to be. It has been overshadowed by pain, disappointment, wrong choices, deception, failure, and fear. Visualize for a moment the best possible you having a conversation with the you that you are now. What would your bestie say? "I know you've had a rough time. I know this person hurt you. We are going to put that behind us. I am who you really are - a wise, beautiful, creation, consistently living in purpose on purpose. And I love who you are."

There is so much wisdom within you that you need to tap into and grasp. This exercise will equip you to have compassion and empathy for yourself and to love you and care about you. Many of us have no idea how to love ourselves. The reality is, it is the only way we will ever determine who we are in Jesus Christ, when we learn to love and appreciate the person inside of us, the person many of us have spent years smothering daily. You have a light in you that was not designed to be under a bushel. Get ready to shine in a way that no opinion, no word, or no past occurrence can dim.

JUST ENOUGH: LET'S TAKE IT PERSONAL

Each of us has areas of deficiency! No matter how polished of a persona we portray, there are areas where we know we need God to fill our voids. Whatever you feel you don't have enough of, is often a place God wants to use your story the most. As 2 Corinthians 12:2 explains *"That is why, for Christ's sake, I delight in weaknesses, in insults, in hardships, in persecutions, in difficulties. For when I am weak, then I am strong."*

The greatest experiences of God's sufficiency and abundance have come from the areas where others might notice deficiency and lack of ability. God's glory shines more in His ability to use us in our *inabilities* than in our *abilities*. The recognition of the recipe for my *enoughness* comes from my acknowledgment of combining the ingredients of what I didn't have enough of with God's recognition of what I had just enough of!

Have you ever been cooking something and didn't have what you thought you needed in the kitchen? Rather than stop and give up on the process of cooking, sometimes you have to put in another ingredient. That unplanned ingredient can often lead to the creation of a new dish, a new taste, and a new masterpiece that is beyond your expectations! Build your own 'Just Enough' recipe of testimonies with me!

THE *ENOUGHNESS* RECIPE FOR ME

My 'Just Enough' Ingredients

I may not have had_____

But I did have_____

And That's Just Enough For God To Use!

- **What I didn't have was an active earthly father in my life. What God gave me was an abundance of love in my family and a mother whose self-less sacrifices are immeasurable.**

My mother, Margaret Rawls, sacrificed as a single parent filing for divorce seven months pregnant with me in the seventies(an unpopular time to do such). She sacrificed her personal life and poured everything into putting me in every extra-curricular and enrichment program available in Jackson, Tennessee. As I grew older, she even financed my matriculation at Clark Atlanta University. Upon my undergraduate graduation, she took an early retirement package in her 40's, paid off my student loans, paid for my wedding, and helped my husband and I with our first apartment as we got married while continuing our education.

Five years into our marriage, when our first child was born, my mother left her hometown, sold her home, gave away her car, and moved to Chicago. She has spent her life serving as a full time "Grammie." It is impossible for me to feel lack from my family foundation. What it looked like I was born missing at birth had been a journey of family and parental abundance at every turn.

- **What I didn't have was a high school graduation. What I did have was a journey of educational accomplishments that only God's grace could have carried me through.**

God's sufficiency continued to outshine my deficiency. My story became a series of failing forward from failure to diploma, from public embarrassment to scholarships, from academic probation to graduation, from self doubt to safe assurance... not self assurance, but safe assurance in my Savior carrying me from victory to victory for His glory.

- **What I didn't have was a flawless journey in and through a life in full time ministry over the past two decades. What I did have was a team of individuals that entered my life in divine timing to pray for me at my weakest points, to lend wisdom to me in areas where I tend to display a lack of wisdom, to protect me from poison not deliver it to me.**

I was once counseling a young lady who was being publicly attacked, and I encouraged her not to read and study comments about herself online. She said that her friends were texting and sending her what was being said about her. I immediately asked her to create a circle who would not forward her fiery darts aimed at her but would shield her from venomous words about her. I cried when she said she could not think of anyone she could trust to do that for her.

I thank God and celebrate the people God has surrounded me with on this imperfect journey I've been on. Not perfect, but protected. In purpose, not poisoned.

I am grateful for my husband and partner in purpose and to my inner circle of protective prayer warriors, I have never felt unsafe to have them as my circle.

- **What I didn't have was perfection, what I did have was protection, and that was just enough for me to know and feel that God is WITH me!**

What are the areas of Just Enough in your life? What are the areas where you may have felt deficiency but God's sufficiency is undeniable in that area? _____

_____

_____

_____

What I didn't have was: _____

_____

_____

But what I did have was: _____

_____

_____

What I didn't have was: _____

_____

_____

But what I did have was: _____

_____

_____

What I didn't have was: _____

_____

_____

_____

But what I did have was: _____

_____

_____

_____

ENOUGH ALREADY

YOUR READINESS FOR LIVING OUT YOUR CALLING

> *"But as His anointing teaches you about all things and as that anointing is real, not counterfeit—just as it has taught you, remain in Him."*
> *1 John 2:27b*

You are enough already because you are anointed. To be anointed means to be empowered with a purpose from the Divine Creator. You have been touched by God. His empowerment in you pre-powers you for everything you will face. Just as some electronics come with a tag that says 'batteries included,' you have been created with power on the inside of you.

Furthermore, when we accept, believe and confess that Jesus Christ is the Son of God, who died for everything we have done wrong and was raised from the dead as the only living God, we have eternal life. We have a new life in Him, and we have the Holy Spirit leading us, guiding us, directing, and protecting us.

The Holy Spirit, a teacher and guide for our lives, is available at all times and brings clarity to our knowing we are enough already. Developing a close personal relationship with the Holy Spirit is essential to understanding the calling God has on our lives. Paul writes in Romans 8:14, *"For those who are led by the Spirit of God are the children of God."* While it sounds wonderful, there is this moment of insecurity – am I led by the Holy Spirit? How does one really know who is leading? Any question we have, God answers in the Bible. His Word is filled with extensive knowledge and solutions. Joshua 1:8 tells us, *"Keep this Book of the Law always on your lips; meditate on it day and night, so that you may be careful to do everything written in it. Then you will be prosperous and successful."*

I recently read a write-up about a well-known and respected man who shared about the Lord daily. People looked to him for advice whether it be in their personal life or professional life. It was said, of all his investments, he had never lost a dime. When anyone asked how he made such wise choices, he would respond, "I do not act until I have heard from the Lord." He brought his issues and possibilities to God. He meditated on the Word of God, and He waited to hear from God. There were times when people became impatient with him and would no longer wait on an answer but moved on to someone else. For this man, that was one way of God answering him – taking the opportunity away. He also said there were times when he wanted to say "yes" but felt "no" in his heart. In all things, the Holy Spirit led him correctly because he waited for the answer even in his work in the financial industry.

It sounds uncommon to some, to include reliance on spiritual disciplines even in secular industry jobs. Meditating on the Word of God is not just a brief reading of scripture – it is allowing it to be a part of your day. It is reading and rereading the Words from God's Bible until the Words speak to you. The Words must take root in our hearts and in so doing, guide us to act accordingly. Some of us do not read the Bible as if It were speaking directly to us. We think of It more as a schoolbook of sorts, and we never see ourselves in the Word. When you read your Bible, tell yourself, "This is what God says about me. This is what God believes I can do. This is what gives me the power to do it."

Learning to accept that we are *enough* just as we are right now begins with a relationship with the Holy Spirit in our lives. Put yourself in agreement with God – agree with what He says about you in His Word. Actively ask the Holy Spirit to direct your steps, to give you clarity, to make the decisions clear to you. We can only walk, talk, and apply the Word of God to our lives when we are in a relationship with the Holy Spirit and seeking His help in our day-to-day experiences. By developing a one-on-one with our Helper – the One Jesus Christ told us about – the One that dwells within us – gives us the ability to remove the doubt, the insecurities, the frustrations, the dark places – and surround ourselves with our Creator. The beauty with connecting with the Holy Spirit is when those doubtful, negative, incorrect words come into our heads – we have the ability to control our thoughts God's way. Do not create a narrative in your mind that does not work for you. Erase those negatives and rewrite powerful stories about yourself.

When searching for God's calling on your life, be aware of the distractions. If a physician gave you a prescription for medication which will keep your heart beating every day, you would take it. In fact, you would probably set several alarms and reminders to make sure you took it every day. We must start seeing essentials such as meditating on God's Word, actively praying, and spending time in worship of Him as that essential pill to keep our hearts beating. Distractions are Satan's favorite weapon. If he can keep you busy, busy, busy, you will slowly become consumed by the world and less aware of the wonderfulness of God.

What things distract you? Distractions are not necessarily bad things. I remember when my children were younger and needed diapers changed, to be fed, or to be held. It was hard to find time to stay in the Word because any spare moment I had, I needed to either sleep, take a nap, or sleep! I learned quickly that in order to be effective at all I was doing, my priority had to be God. Spending time with Him was key to everything that I did. Spending time with God can look differently in different seasons. In some seasons, my devotion time is in the car. In some seasons, I'm listening to the Word of God on audio while getting ready for bed.

Some distractions are not good. We can be distracted by material wealth and our desire to gain it - all! We can be distracted by our performance and the level of praise we receive from other people. Some distractions are how we are perceived by other people and how we view ourselves. School, career, personal relationships, unhealthy habits, all qualify as distractions which keep us from Him.

As you plan out your day, and I recommend you become a scheduler, be intentional about time with God. Ask that He bring to you His Will for your life each day. Know when your best time of day for focused prayer and reading of the Word is. For some morning people, you may have your best time with God by waking up earlier than everyone around you. For my fellow night owls, you may gain the most insight at midnight. Know what your best time is.

Be direct with the Holy Spirit for clear direction and guidance in decision making throughout the day. Divine interactions and appointments center your day when you give your schedule to Him. Ephesians 6:11 tells us to, *"Put on the full armor of God, so that you can take your stand against the devil's schemes."* These are not small words and should not be taken lightly. I make it a common practice to put on the *full armor of God* each day. *"For our struggle is not against flesh and blood, but against the rulers, against the evil in the heavenly realms"* (12). The battles we face are very real against spiritual forces of evil.

"Therefore, put on the full armor of God, so that when the day of evil comes, you may be able to stand your ground, and after you have done everything, to stand" (13).

Therefore — whenever I read this word, I sit up and take note. Therefore is a word which denotes action and one that should be taken seriously. Therefore, I buckle my belt of truth around my waist and make sure my breastplate of righteousness is in place. That belt of truth will force me to the Words of God about me. It will help focus my thoughts on *"...whatever is **true**, whatever is noble, whatever is right, whatever is pure, whatever is lovely, whatever is admirable–if anything is excellent or praiseworthy–think about such things"* - Philippians 4:8. As you are dressing yourself, secure that belt around your waist so that the truth of our Heavenly Father walks with you.

Next, place the breastplate of righteousness on your chest to guard your heart. Proverbs 4:23 tells us, *"Above all else, guard your heart, it is the wellspring of life."* It matters what we read; what we look at; who we speak with; and what we listen to. By constantly desiring earthly things only, we let our guard down. We think carnal thoughts and act in ways that are not Holy Spirit led. We convince ourselves and justify our actions by believing God's Word is no longer relevant. But, God's word is timeless.

Reach down and hold on to your feet. Ask the Holy Spirit to direct your steps. To keep you at peace as the day unfolds. To know the calling God has on your life, you must commit to giving Him control and access to your day. While it might seem awkward, it will put a visual reminder of Who turns your foot, step-by-step, to keep you on the path He has chosen for you. Psalm 23:3 tells us, "…*He guides me along the right paths for His name's sake.*"

We have to be committed to giving God "our best self." Not the leftover self. Not the one who has worked all day, watched TV, tended to Social Media, and closes his/her eyes to a realization – "Oh yea – I forgot to pray." Think of it this way. When I was going to see my husband, Charles, when we were just dating, I spent days thinking of the right look. Our whole courtship was a long distance relationship (before Facetime), so when I would finally get to see him, I wanted it to be memorable. My nails were done. My hair in place; perfume; jewelry; perfect shoes. Never would I get to the time that I was going to see him, and my preparation for that day be an afterthought with thrown on clothes. How much more should we do for our Savior? We should prepare for our time with Him regularly and meet each moment with expectation.

His plan for our lives can be revealed the clearest when we are willing to give Him our best – right here – right now – just as we are. Because of this, we have to learn to trust God and His Word. It is through His Word that He will reveal His plan for your life in each season of your life, and you will hear your calling.

A friend of mine told me a story about her brother. He had several children and had to move around a good bit because of his job. The youngest son struggled making friends, fitting in, making good grades, staying out of adventurous situations… you know the struggles young teenage boys can have. As he grew older, he just made it out of high school with a diploma, got fired from several jobs, and ended up on his dad's couch again – defeated and unwilling to do anything. My friend would say, "You need to kick that boy out! Show him some tough love. He needs to get his life together, and he won't do this if you are always bailing him out."

A few years ago, I saw an announcement of this same boy graduating from medical school as he's becoming an anesthesiologist. How could this be? I had lost touch with the family but still, it seemed this boy – now man – was heading for trouble – not college much less medical school! I, of course, called my friend elated and eager to hear how things turned around. Her words were simple – my brother never gave up on him. Never. This intrigued me. What was his story?

He said on his post about his graduation, "My dad never stopped telling me he believed in me. He never stopped saying – I know God has plans for your life. When you are ready, you will listen."

What a beautiful, real story, and one we can take to heart. See, God never stops believing that we will come back to the person He created us to be. He is waiting and ready for us to listen to Him and allow Him to guide us down the path He has intended for us to be on all along. It starts with an acceptance of who we are right now. Remember those hugs I told you about? Now is the time to give yourself one.

Fred Rogers had a television show for children on PBS called *Mr. Roger's Neighborhood.* Some of you may have watched him and some of you may have just heard of him with the release of the movie about his life; but, he would end the show with a simple song which he had written called "It's you I like."

> *It's you I like,*
> *It's not the things you wear,*
> *It's not the way you do your hair*
> *But it's you I like*
> *The way you are right now,*
> *The way down deep inside you*
> *Not the things that hide you,*
> *Not your toys*
> *They're just beside you.*
> *But it's you I like*
> *Every part of you.*
> *Your skin, your eyes, your feelings*
> *Whether old or new.*
> *I hope that you'll remember*
> *Even when you're feeling blue*
> *That it's you I like,*
> *It's you yourself*
> *It's you.*
> *It's you I like.*

Written by Fred Rogers | © 1971, Fred M. Rogers

What I'd like for you to do right now is to insert the word "love" for "like". I can imagine God singing a similar song to you, "It's you I love. It's not the things you wear. It's not the way you do your hair, but it's you I love. The way you are RIGHT NOW. The way down deep inside you, not the things that hide you, not your stuff, it's just beside you. But it's you I love. EVERY part of you. Your skin, your eyes, your feelings whether old or new. I hope that you'll remember, even when you're feeling blue. That it's you I love, It's you yourself, It's you. It's you I LOVE." – GOD

It starts with the belief that God loves you just as you are. In 2 Timothy 1:6-7, Paul tells us, *"For this reason I remind you to fan into flame the gift of God, which is in you through the laying on of my hands, for God gave us a spirit not of fear but of power and love and self-control."*

What are your gifts, talents, desires, passions? Become prayerfully aware of your uniqueness. Ask God to help you discover ways to use those gifts and talents for the benefit of His Kingdom and the fulfillment of your creation. Some people think that our work for the Lord needs to be in the Church. Others think it's Evangelizing, going on Mission Trips, or working for a Non-profit. Do you realize it could be right in your household or at work or at school? It could be a calling to be a mother, teacher, coach, mentor, friend. Kingdom work isn't just about preaching, Kingdom work is anything that helps bring this world back to the place God created it to be.

Are you ready to be who God says you are? It starts with you. It begins with your releasing the hold that tells us we are destined to please society. It begins with giving the controls to God. What is important to God? I want you to remember, it doesn't happen overnight because we are too stubborn and too set in our ways. But through our connection and relationship with God; by being proactive every day in our prayers and meditation on the Word; and by being doers of the Word of God, we can change. When I say change, I do not mean who we are – I mean how we think – how we perceive ourselves – how we see our circumstances – how we view our lives - and how we remove the labels others have attached to us.

You are loved with a love you cannot fathom or comprehend by God, your Creator. You are going to do great things for the Kingdom of God. I want to thank you for finding your *enoughness* in Jesus Christ because in so doing, you and I allow the anointing and empowerment of the Holy Spirit to do each task He has asked us to do. You are going to realize what you need to give-up in your life and who you need to walk away from. People will start seeing you differently and wondering what has happened in your life. You will find meaning and purpose in your everyday walk with Him. It has been a privilege to spend time with you on your journey to find who you ALREADY are. I praise God that we are *enough* in Him!

ENOUGH ALREADY: LET'S TAKE IT PERSONAL

Have you ever heard someone talk about "when not to pray"? It sounds unspiritual and unspirited, but there are times when we have to say Amen to our prayers and start doing!

What are the actionable steps now that you know you are ENOUGH and you have the ENOUGHNESS you need in Him?

A few years ago, I had an opportunity to get another additional degree title through taking three more classes over the course of three more semesters. I considered it heavily as I grew up in a context where education is esteemed.

As much as I wanted to do it just because of the innate determination and drive that I have for certain pursuits, I could not get peace with it. I felt God leading me saying, "It's time to move from preparation to performance."

We can't wait to arrive at a place of perfection for participation in our purpose.

Even in completing this book, it's been a constant pushing through feelings of not *enoughness* gnawing at my knowing!

We must break the cycle of prideful procrastination and the pause that perfectionism causes and GO! BE! DO!

GO IN THE AREA OF YOUR ENOUGHNESS!

BE ALL IN YOUR ENOUGHNESS!

DO ALL YOU ARE CALLED TO DO IN YOUR ENOUGHNESS!

On Your Mark! Get Set! Go! Be! Do!

What's Stalling You In Your Starter's Blocks? _____

_____

_____

How has pride stopped you from going and being ALL READY? _____

_____

_____

How has perfectionism stopped you from going and being ALL READY? _____

_____

_____

How has procrastination stopped you from going and being ALL READY? _____

_____

_____

How have people stopped you from going and being ALL READY? _____

_____

_____

How has personal doubt stopped you from going and being ALL READY? _____

_____

_____

How have politics or policies in your industry stopped you from going and being

ALL READY? _____

_____

_____

_____

How has your perception of yourself stopped you from going and being

ALL READY? _____

_____

_____

_____

ENOUGH SAID

///

Through this journey, through all of the areas where I could be *Never Enough*, God showed me that I *Had Enough*. The Enemy needed to know *Enough is Enough,* and I told him just that. In spite of what I'm not, I've got *Just Enough* for God to still use me. Because of this I confess, decree, and declare that I'm *Enough Already,* I'm *Enough,* and I'm *ALL ready!*

Now, let's speak these scriptures together, discovering that through God's Word, there's been *Enough Said* about you for you to believe in your *ENOUGHNESS* in HIM! The most powerful weapon we have is praying scriptures by faith. Scripture is filled with declarations for you, about you, and your *enoughness!*

As you speak scripture, I believe that your feelings of inadequacy will be replaced with feelings of boldness and faith-filled *ENOUGHNESS*!

The Bible provides us with hope in knowing that there has been *ENOUGH SAID* about you in God's Word to fill the voids and empty places in your life with abundance.

So, together, let's say what He says about us!

I AM BEAUTIFUL *ENOUGH* BECAUSE

Psalm 139:14 *declares:*

"I praise you because I am fearfully and wonderfully made; your works are wonderful, I know that full well."

1 Peter 1:23

"I am born again - spiritually transformed, renewed and set apart for God's purpose through the living and everlasting Word of God."

2 Corinthians 5:17

"I am a new creation in Christ."

Genesis 1:27

"So God created mankind in His own image, in the image of God He created them; male and female He created them."

Ephesians 3:11

"He has made everything beautiful in its time. He has also set eternity in the human heart; yet, no one can fathom what God has done from beginning to end."

Proverbs 3:15-18

"She is more precious than rubies; nothing you desire can compare with her. Long life is in her right hand; in her left hand are riches and honor. Her ways are pleasant ways, and all her paths are peaceful. She is a tree of life to those who take hold of her; those who hold her fast will be blessed."

2 Corinthians 5:20

> "I am an ambassador of Christ."

1 Peter 2:9

> *"I am part of a chosen generation, a royal priesthood, a Holy nation, a purchased people."*

1 Corinthians 5:21

> *"My body is a temple of the Holy Spirit; I belong to Him."*

Genesis 1:31

> *"And God saw all that He made, and behold, it was very good."*

I AM EQUIPPED *ENOUGH* BECAUSE

Philippians 4:13 *declares*

"I can do all things through Him Who gives me strength."

Colossians 1:11

"I am strengthened with all power according to His glorious might."

2 Corinthians 3:5

"Not that we are competent in ourselves to claim anything for ourselves, but our competence comes from God."

Philippians 1:6

"And I am sure of this, that He who began a good work in you will bring it to completion at the day of Jesus Christ."

Phillippians 2:13

"...for it is God who works in you, both to will and to work for His good pleasure."

Hebrews 13:20-21

"Now may the God of peace, who through the blood of the eternal covenant brought back from the dead our Lord Jesus, that great Shepherd of the sheep, equip you with everything good for doing his will, and may he work in us what is pleasing to him, through Jesus Christ, to whom be glory for ever and ever. Amen."

1 Peter 5:10

"And the God of all grace, who called you to his eternal glory in Christ, after you have suffered a little while, will himself restore you and make you strong, firm and steadfast."

Psalm 138:8

*"The Lord will vindicate me; Your love, Lord, endures forever - do not aban-
don the works of Your hands."*

2 Thessalonians 1:1

*"With this in mind, we constantly pray for you, that our God may make you
worthy of his calling, and that by his power he may bring to fruition your every
desire for goodness and your every deed prompted by faith."*

2 Thessalonians 3

*"But the Lord is faithful, and he will strengthen you and protect you from the
evil one. We have confidence in the Lord that you are doing and will continue
to do the things we command."*

I AM RESILIENT *ENOUGH* BECAUSE

Psalm 46:5 *declares*

"God is within her, she will not fall."

1 Chronicles 28:20

"...Be strong and courageous, and do the work. Do not be afraid or discouraged, for the Lord God, my God, is with you. He will not fail you or forsake you..."

1 Chronicles 28:20

"Therefore, my dear brothers and sisters, stand firm. Let nothing move you. Always give yourselves fully to the work of the Lord, because you know that your labor in the Lord is not in vain."

Deuteronomy 31:6

"Be strong and courageous. Do not be afraid or terrified because of them, for the LORD your God goes with you; He will never leave you nor forsake you."

John 14:27

"Peace I leave with you; my peace I give you. I do not give to you as the world gives. Do not let your hearts be troubled and do not be afraid."

Psalm 56:3-4

"When I am afraid, I put my trust in you. In God, whose word I praise - in God, I trust and am not afraid. What can mere mortals do to me?"

2 Timothy 1:7

"For the Spirit God gave us does not make us timid, but gives us power, love, and self-discipline."

Joshua 1:9

"Have I not commanded you? Be strong and courageous. Do not be afraid; do not be discouraged, for the LORD your God will be with you wherever you go."

Ephesians 6:10-14

"Finally, be strong in the Lord, relying on His mighty strength. Put on the whole armor of God so that you may be able to stand firm against the Devil's strategies. For our struggle is not against the Devil's strategies. For our struggle is not against human opponents, but against rulers, authorities, cosmic powers in the darkness around us, and evil spiritual forces in the Heavenly realm. For this reason, take up the whole armor of God so that you may be able to take a stand whenever evil comes. And when you have done everything you could, you will be able to stand firm. Stand firm, therefore, having fastened the belt of truth around your waist, and having put on the breastplate of righteousness."

Romans 8:28

"And we know that in all things God works for the good of those who love him, who[a] have been called according to his purpose."

I AM STRONG *ENOUGH* BECAUSE

Psalm 28:76 *declares*

"The Lord is my strength and my shield."

Psalm 46:1

"God is our refuge and strength, an ever-present help in trouble."

Proverbs 18:10

"The name of the Lord is a fortified tower; the righteous run to it and are safe."

Nehemiah 8:10

"Do not grieve, for the joy of the Lord is your strength."

1 Chronicles 16:11

"Look to the Lord, and His strength; seek His face always."

Deuteronomy 20:4

"For the LORD your God is the one who goes with you to fight for you against your enemies to give you victory."

Exodus 15:2

"The Lord is my strength and my defense; He has become my salvation. He is my God, and I will praise Him, my father's God, and I will exalt Him."

John 16:33

"I have told you these things, so that in me you may have peace. In this world you will have trouble. But take heart! I have overcome the world."

Isaiah 41:10

"So do not fear, for I am with you; do not be dismayed, for I am your God. I will strengthen you and help you; I will uphold you with my righteous right hand."

Psalm 27:10

"The LORD is my light and my salvation— whom shall I fear? The LORD is the stronghold of my life— of whom shall I be afraid?"

I AM UNCONDITIONALLY LOVED
ENOUGH BECAUSE

Romans 5:8 *declares*

"I loved you at your darkest."

Jeremiah 31:3

"The Lord appeared to us in the past, saying: "I have loved you with an everlasting love; I have drawn you with unfailing kindness.""

John 3:16

"For God so loved the world that He gave His one and only Son, that whoever believes in Him shall not perish but have eternal life."

1 John 3:1

"See what great love the Father has lavished on us, that we should be called children of God! And that is what we are! The reason the world does not know us is that it did not know Him."

John 14:21

"Whoever has my commands and keeps them is the one who loves Me. The one who loves Me will be loved by My Father, and I too will love them and show Myself to them."

Romans 5:5

"And hope does not put us to shame, because God's love has been poured out into our hearts through the Holy Spirit, who has been given to us."

1 John 4:9-10

"This is how God showed His love among us: He sent His one and only Son into the world that we might live through Him. This is love: not that we loved

God, but that He loved us and sent His Son as an atoning sacrifice for our sins."

Romans 8:37-38

"No, in all these things we are more than conquerors through Him Who loved us. For I am sure that neither death nor life, nor angels nor rulers, nor things present nor things to come, nor powers, nor height nor depth, nor anything else in all creation, will be able to separate us from the love of God in Christ Jesus our Lord."

Psalm 103:8

"The Lord is merciful and gracious, slow to anger and abounding in steadfast love."

Psalm 103:11

"For as high as the Heavens are above the Earth, so great is His steadfast love toward those who fear Him."

I AM PROTECTED *ENOUGH* BECAUSE

Psalm 62:5-6 declares

"Only God gives inward peace, and I depend on Him. God alone is the mighty rock that keeps me safe, and He is the fortress where I feel secure."

2 Thessalonians 3:3

"*But the Lord is faithful, and He will strengthen you and protect you from the evil one."*

Isaiah 41:10

"So do not fear, for I am with you; do not be dismayed, for I am your God. I will strengthen you and help you; I will uphold you with my righteous right hand."

Psalm 5:11

"But let all who take refuge in you be glad; let them ever sing for joy. Spread your protection over them, that those who love your name may rejoice in you."

Psalm 34:19

"The righteous person may have many troubles, but the Lord delivers him from them all;"

Psalm 46:1

"God is our refuge and strength, an ever-present help in trouble."

Psalm 59:1

"Deliver me from my enemies, O God; be my fortress against those who are attacking me."

Psalm 138:7

"Though I walk in the midst of trouble, you preserve my life. You stretch out your hand against the anger of my foes; with your right hand you."

2 Corinthians 4:8-9

"We are hard pressed on every side, but not crushed; perplexed, but not in despair; persecuted, but not abandoned; struck down, but not destroyed."

Psalm 2

"The Lord is my shepherd, I lack nothing. He makes me lie down in green pastures, He leads me beside quiet waters, He refreshes my soul. He guides me along the right paths for His name's sake. Even though I walk through the darkest valley, I will fear no evil, for You are with me; Your rod and Your staff, they comfort me. You prepare a table before me in the presence of my enemies. You anoint my head with oil; my cup overflows. Surely your goodness and love will follow me all the days of my life, and I will dwell in the house of the Lord forever."

I AM FEARLESS *ENOUGH* BECAUSE

2 Timothy 1:7 declares

"For the Spirit that God gave us does not make us timid, but gives us power, love, and self-discipline."

Daniel 6:26-27

"For He is the living God and He endures forever; His kingdom will not be destroyed. His dominion will never end.' He rescues and He saves; He performs signs and wonders in the Heavens and on the Earth. He has rescued Daniel from the power of the lions."

Hebrews 10:35-36

"*So do not throw away your confidence; it will be richly rewarded. You need to persevere so that when you have done the will of God, you will receive what He has promised."*

Jeremiah 1:8

"Do not be afraid of them, For I am with you to deliver you," declares the LORD.

Proverbs 31:25

"Strength and dignity are her clothing, And she smiles at the future."

Exodus 14:14

"The LORD will fight for you while you keep silent."

Proverbs 30:5

"Every word of God is tested; He is a shield to those who take refuge in Him."

Job 41:33

"Nothing on earth is like Him, One made without fear."

Hebrews 13:6

"...so that we confidently say, "The Lord is my Helper. I will not be afraid. What will man do to me?"

Luke 1:45

"And blessed is she who believed that there would be a fulfillment of what had been spoken to her by the Lord."

I AM TRIUMPHANT *ENOUGH* BECAUSE

2 Chronicles 20:15 tells me

"The battle is not mine, but God's!"

1 John 5:4

"For everyone born of God overcomes the world. This is the victory that has overcome the world, even our faith."

1 Corinthians 10:13

"No temptation has overtaken you except what is common to mankind. And God is faithful; He will not let you be tempted beyond what you can bear. But when you are tempted, He will also provide a way out so that you can endure it."

Psalm 3:8

"From the Lord comes deliverance. May your blessing be on your people."

Proverbs 21:31

"The horse is made ready for the day of battle, but victory rests with the Lord."

1 Corinthians 15:57

"But thanks be to God! He gives us the victory through our Lord Jesus Christ."

2 Corinthians 2:14

"But thanks be to God, who in Christ always leads us in triumphal procession, and through us spreads the fragrance of the knowledge of Him everywhere."

Romans 6:14

"For sin will have no dominion over you, since you are not under law but under grace."

Isaiah 55:11

"So shall My Word be that goes out from My mouth; it shall not return to Me empty, but it shall accomplish that which I purpose, and shall succeed in the thing for which I sent it."

Romans 8:2

"For the law of the Spirit of life has set you free in Christ Jesus from the law of sin and death."

ENOUGH SAID: LET'S TAKE IT PERSONAL

Take a device that records audio, whether that be an app on your phone like 'voice notes' or an old-fashioned tape recorder that you saved from years ago. Record your voice saying the ENOUGH declarations above. Read it, record it, and replay it. Repeat! Read it, record it, and replay it!

If there is a particular area in your life in which you have felt challenged in your *enoughness*, add to the list of scriptures and declarations above.

PERSONALIZE YOUR 'ENOUGH SAID' LIST

I am _____ENOUGH because

Scripture tells me in_____ that _____

_____

_____

I am _____ENOUGH because

Scripture tells me in_____ that _____

_____

_____

I am _____ENOUGH because

Scripture tells me in_____ that _____

_____

_____

I am _____ENOUGH because

Scripture tells me in_____ that _____

_____

_____

I am _____ENOUGH because

Scripture tells me in_____ that _____

_____

_____

I am _____ENOUGH because

Scripture tells me in_____ that _____

_____

_____

ACKNOWLEDGMENTS

Thank you to my family, friends, Fellowship MIssionary Baptist Church Family of Chicago, Illinois.

Thank you to my family: the Rawls, Fuller, and Jenkins crews.

I can't celebrate my husband and mother ENOUGH for the level of support that surrounds me.

To my incredible family, who for all of my life, whether near or far have always made me feel like I have more than enough to face everything that comes my way, I appreciate you!

Thank you to my sister friends, who have been in the delivery room with me for this project: Phillis, Stephanie, Robin, Anika, Allyson, Abbie, Lori, Shameka, Brittney, Tenitra, Tiffany, Adrienne, Jamell, Lisa, Bev and Ms. Monica! I so appreciate you. Thank you to all of my Ministry Mates who chant to me, "I know you can, I know you can! Thank You Gloria, Erica, Marcie, Latonia, Cleo, Dr. Sheila Bailey and Rev. Tonia Johnson.

To The Late Dr. Lois Evans, your words of encouragement echo in my heart.

Thank you to my Fellowship Church Family who have literally been a family to me throughout my journey in ministry over the past two decades. I love you and appreciate every prayer, every word of encouragement and every way you have pulled for me! Whether you were in my presence encouraging me or in my absence promoting and protecting me, I sincerely appreciate you.

To the Evans family who continues to be our family, I love you!

To The team who has traveled near and far to serve alongside whatever I was doing in that season, I can't thank you enough, Ms. Monica, Shataka, Alicia, Linda, Ms. T and the late Ms. Niecey.

To Pastor Sharpe and Lady Bri, I thank you for your ongoing love and support!

ABOUT THE AUTHOR

Tara Rawls Jenkins, Ed.D. is a creative communicator of God's word. Her messages often infuse spoken word, music and dance, utilizing secular cultural references to explain scriptural principles.

She is a graduate of Clark-Atlanta University with a Bachelor of Arts in Mass Media Arts, Moody Bible Institute with a Master of Arts in Biblical Studies and Southern Baptist Theological Seminary with a Doctorate of Education in Leadership.

With a passion to see women, wives and girls empowered, Tara enjoys convening faith lifting events.

Tara is also the founder of MinistryMates.org, an organization that equips ministers' wives and pastors' wives for ministry.

Tara resides with her songwriting/recording artist husband, Charles and their three extraordinary children Princess (17), Paris (15), and Charles III (11).